Tax-Wise
Business Ownership

Tax-Wise
Business Ownership

Comprehensive, up-to-date
tax strategies for staying afloat in
today's economy and keeping more
of what you earn!

Toby Mathis, Esq.

ANDERSON LAW GROUP

www.andersonadvisors.com

Published by Anderson Business Advisors
3225 McLeod Drive
Las Vegas, NV 89121

This book is intended to be informative and to aid in the education of its audience. Although the author and publisher are engaged in rendering legal, financial, tax preparation, and other professional services—this book is no substitute for legal, accounting, or other professional services. Because laws vary from state to state and are constantly changing, readers who require expert assistance or legal advice, should seek the services of competent professionals should.

The author and publisher specifically disclaim responsibility for any liability, loss, or risk, personal or otherwise, which may be incurred as a consequence, directly or indirectly, of the use and/or application of the contents of this book.

Copyright © 2016 by Anderson Law Group, PLLC.
All rights reserved.

ISBN: 978-0-9728128-6-3   Hardback
ISBN: 978-0-9728128-7-0   Paperback Edition
ISBN: 978-0-9728128-5-6   ePub/ebook edition
ISBN: 978-0-9797860-9-9   Mobi/Kindle/ebook edition

Get the right digital edition for your favorite eReader: The ePub for iPads and B&N Nook, and Mobi for Kindle and the Sony eReader.

Without limiting the rights under copyright reserved above, no part of this book may be reproduced in any form or by any electronic or mechanical means, including information storage and retrieval systems, without permission in writing from the publisher, except by a reviewer who may quote brief passages in a published review.

Printed in the United States of America

10 9 8 7 6 5 4 3 2 1

About the Author

Toby Mathis is a small business owner, real estate investor and attorney. He has had companies on the *Inc.* Magazine list of fastest growing companies on three different occasions, been the President of a Chamber "Business of the Year" and "Best Places to Work," is a Board member of the Las Vegas Chapter of Entrepreneurs Organization, and owns real estate from coast to coast in the United States. Toby is a true entrepreneur.

Prior to joining Anderson Law Group as a partner in 1999, Toby was a small business owner and general law practitioner—advising many Seattle-based companies. His focus was always on helping small business and their owners.

Since joining Anderson Law Group, Toby has authored countless articles on legal and financial planning and coauthored several books and educational programs designed to teach individuals how to run small businesses. He does not believe you can accurately teach a subject unless you actively engage in the subject you are teaching. As a result he remains active in all aspects of the ventures in which he invests.

Dedicated to all small business owners in the United States. A wise man once said, "Be self-employed and you only have to work half the time . . . you even get to decide which 12 hours of every day you have to work."

TOBY MATHIS, ESQ.

Contents

Preface xxi

Overview 1
    An Innovative Guide 1
    Scope 2
    Don't Go It Alone 2
    How This Book Is Organized 3
        Chapter Structure 5
        Point of Emphasis 6
        Treatment 6
    The Challenge 7

Chapter 1—The Basics 9
    Relax 9
    Communicate 10
    The US Tax System 11
        The IRC 12
        The IRS 13
        On a Personal Level 14
        Responsibility 15
        Collection, Collection, Collection 15
    Staying Off the Radar Screen 17
    Complexity Brings Opportunity 19

Code of Conduct Relief 20

Income and Expenses 20
  Dollar-for-Dollar Deductions 22
  When in Doubt, Deduct 22

Audits 23
  Audit Period 24
  Record Keeping 24
  Audit Representation 24
  Selecting a Representative 27
  Protecting Yourself 27

Moving On 29

Chapter 2—The Tax Foundation 31

Tax Planning 31

The Taxpayer 32

Classifying Tax-Wise Strategies 32

Tax-Wise Income Strategies 33
  Definition of Income 33
  Income Exclusions 35
  Income Categories 35
  Capital Gains and Losses 37
  Passive Income and Losses 39

Tax-Wise Expense Strategies 40
  Expenses Categories 40
  Definition of Business Expense 41

The Power of Business Deductions 43
  Business Startup Example 46
  Overcoming Your Reluctance 52
  Business Profit Requirement—the Truth 53
  Holdbacks 54
  Know How to Ask the Question 55

Chapter 3—The Business Framework 57

Defining Parameters 59
- Flow-Through Taxation 59
- Limited Liability 60

Legal Structures 60

Sole Proprietorship 61
- Definition 61
- Operations 62
- Liability 62
- Taxation 63
- Changing the Business 68
- Ending the Business 69
- Death and Taxes 69
- Sole Proprietorship Example 69
- Advantages of Sole Proprietorships 71
- Disadvantages of Sole Proprietorships 71

Partnerships 72
- Definition 72
- Legal Status 73
- Agreements 73
- Taxation of Partnerships 74

General Partnership 75
- Operations 76
- Liabilities 76
- Taxation 76
- General Partnership Example 77
- Advantages of General Partnerships 78
- Disadvantages of General Partnerships 78

Limited Partnership 79
- General Partners 79
- Limited Partners 79
- Formation 80
- Taxation 80

Expanded Uses 81
Advantages of Limited Partnerships 83
Disadvantages of Limited Partnerships 83

Corporations 84
Definition 84
Formation 85
Operation 85
Expense Deductions 86
Liability 88

C Corporation 89
Taxation 90
Double Taxation 90
State Tax 91
Special Characteristics 92
Corporate Income Tax Rates 93
Advantages of C Corporations 93
Disadvantages of C Corporations 94

S Corporation 94
Qualifications 95
Taxation 95
Advantages of S Corporations 97
Disadvantages of S Corporations 98

Personal Service Corporation 98
Qualifying 99
Taxation 100

Limited Liability Company (LLC) 101
Formation 101
Liability 103
Taxation 104
Advantages of LLCs 105
Disadvantages of LLCs 106

Joint Venture 107

Entity Structuring 107

Contents   **xiii**

    Control Issues   107
    Control Issue Comparison   108
    Liability Issues   109
    Liability Issue Comparison   110
    Tax Issues   111
    Tax Issue Comparison   112
    Divide and Conquer   112

Chapter 4—The Language   117

Accounting   117
    Period (Tax Year)   118
    Methods   119

Assets   120
    Business Assets   120
    Capital Assets   121
    Nonbusiness Assets   121
    Real Property   122
    Fair Market Value (FMV)   122

Basis   122
    Cost Basis   122
    Gift (Transferred) Basis   123
    Bartered Basis   124
    Inherited Basis   125
    Exchanged (Substituted) Basis   126
    Converted Basis   127
    Adjusted Basis   127

Deducting Expenses   130
    Capital Expenses   130
    Deductible Expenses   131
    Nondeductible Expenses   131
    Timing   132
    Depreciation   132
    Section 179 Deductions   138
    Bonus Depreciation   139

Amortization 140
Depletion 141
Date of Service 142
Useful Life 142

Deduction Categories 142
Current Expenses 143
Depreciable Assets 145
Amortizable Costs 146

Deducting Limitations 147
Hobby Loss Rules 148
Passive Activity Rules 152
At-Risk Rules 154

Record Keeping 155
General Guidelines 155
Expense Records 156
Special Situations 157
Tax Returns 157

Tax Filing 158
Amended Returns 158
Nonpayment 158
Penalties and Interest 159
IRS Challenges 160

Chapter 5—Deductions 161

Accident and Health Benefits 162
S Corporation Shareholders 163

Affordable Care Act 163
Self-Employed 164
Employers with Fewer Than 25 Employees 166
Employers with Up to 50 Employees 170
Employers with 50 or More Employees 171

Accounting and Bookkeeping 172

Achievement Awards 174

Adoption Assistance   174

Advertising   175

Appraisals   175

Assessments   176

Associations—Clubs   178

Athletic Facilities   178

Attorney Fees   179

Autos   180

Bad Debts   180

Bank Fees   183

Bartering   184

Bonuses   185

Business Set Up Expenses   186
   Startup Costs   187
   Corporation Organizational Costs   188
   Partnership Organizational Costs   189

Charitable Contributions   191

Cleaning Services   192

Communications
—Telephone and Cell Phone Fees   193

Computer Software   193

Computers and Peripherals   194

Conventions   194

Credit Cards   195

De Minimis (Minimal) Benefits   196

Dependent Care Assistance   197

Deposits   198

Directors' Fees   200

Discounts 200

Dividends—Corporate Distributions 201
    Ordinary Dividends 202
    Capital Gain Dividends 203
    Nontaxable Dividends 203

Draws 205
    Sole Proprietorships, Partnerships, LLCs 205
    C Corporations 205
    S Corporations 206

Education 206
    Education Assistance Programs 207
    Work-Related Education and Training 209

Employees' Pay 211

Entertainment 214

Family Employees 216

Fringe Benefits 218

Furniture and Fixtures 221

Home Office 221
    The Simplified Method 222

Independent Contractors 223

Information Systems
    — **Computers and Peripherals** 224

Insurance 226
    Liability and Malpractice Insurance 226
    Life Insurance 226
    Vehicle Insurance 227

Intangible Property 227

Intellectual Property 227

Interest
    — **Loans, Mortgages, and Credit Cards** 228

Internet
— **Access and Online Service Fees** 229

Leases 230

Licenses 230

Manufacturing Equipment 230

Materials and Supplies 230

Meals 231
Entertainment Expense Meals 232
Fringe Benefit Meals 232
Business Travel Meals 235
Promotional Meals 236

Office Furniture, Fixtures, and Equipment 236

Office Services 237

Postage 238

Product Development 238

Production (Manufacturing) Equipment 238

Promotion (Advertising) 240

Property Improvements 242

Publications
— **Business, Professional, and Trade** 243

Real Estate 244

Reimbursements 245

Rent
— **Lease Payments** 247
Inclusions 247
Restrictions 248

Repairs 249

Royalties 250

Scholarships 251

Contents

Section 179 Intangibles   251

Seminars   251

Shipping and Freight   254

Stock Options   255

Supplies   256

Tax Credits   256

Tax Penalties   257

Taxes   257
    Alternative Minimum Tax (AMT)   257
    Payroll Taxes   258
    Property Taxes—Inventory   259
    Property Taxes—Personal Property   259
    Property Taxes—Real Estate   260
    Sales Tax   261
    Self-Employment Tax   261
    Unemployment Insurance Tax   263
    Use Tax   263

Tools   264

Travel   264
    Defining Business Travel   264
    Deductible Expenses   265
    Travel in the United States   267
    Travel Outside of the United States   268

Vehicles   270
    Actual Expenses   271
    Standard Mileage Rate   272
    Vehicle Deduction Limits   274

Chapter 6—Tax Deferral   279

Business-Sponsored Retirement Plans   280
    SEP Plans   281
    SIMPLE Plans   283

       Qualified Plans   286
       Nonqualified Plans   293

Business Structure Limitations   295

Individual Retirement Accounts   296
       Traditional Individual Retirement Accounts (IRAs)   296
       Roth IRAs   298

Health Savings Accounts (HSAs)   299
       HDHP Deductible Limits   299
       Employer Contributions   300
       Distributions   301
       Flexibility   301

Health Reimbursement Arrangements (HRAs)   302

Appendix A—Useful Tax Information   305

Possible Business Deductions   305

Partnerships   306

C Corporations   307

S Corporations   308

Estates, Trusts, and Gifts   309
       Unified Credit   310
       Gift Tax   310
       Estate Tax   312
       Estate & Gift Tax Rates   314

Personal Income Tax Rates   315

Appendix B—Business Tax Strategies   317

Business Structure   317

Income and Expenses   317

Compensation   318

Tax Deferral   319

Family Employees   319

Preface

Have you ever been to Disney World? If so, you may have traveled to Orlando by plane. When you leave the Orlando airport, you will find plenty of signs that show you how to get to Mickey and his friends at Disney World. If you follow the signs, not only will you find the mouse, but you will also find that you have to stop periodically and pay tolls. What you may not be aware of, is that the tolls are voluntary. This is not to say that you can blow through the gates without paying, but there are non-toll roads that will also take you to Disney World—it is just that the signs only point to the toll roads.

Life imitates the way to Disney World in many respects. First, convenient signs often hide a hidden agenda—one that can prove costly for you. Second, the easy way is often the most expensive. Finally, there is often a better way, a cheaper way, a way that you may not be aware of—that's when it pays to know a "local" or a guide who can show you the way that is not known to those who do not have such knowledge.

You do not know what you do not know.

I first published this book in 2003. It took me several years to write the first version as it proved to be more difficult than I anticipated. The tax laws are constantly evolving and congress is in the habit of adding to the laws on a constant basis.

Since this book was first published, there have been many tax acts passed and new court opinions issued, but the core of the book remains unaffected. While the wording of the tax laws may change, the underlying premise of tax-wise planning remains unchanged: know enough to look at things from a different perspective and know where to find answers to the questions that will undoubtedly arise when you do start looking at this differently.

You will find that this book contains many of the answers to the questions you will begin to develop as you run your business. You will also find that the book may cause you to ask more questions of your accountants, attorneys and other advisors. This is good. It leads to discourse that should prove to be in your best interests.

Be wary of those professionals who refuse to talk openly about your tax picture. They may be in their own comfort zone and wish to keep you there with them. As is the case with most things worthwhile in life, anything worth doing generally requires a little work. Well, if you are going to save money on taxes, you are going to have to work at it. You need professionals who will help you along the way, not hold you back. Find encouraging professionals who are willing to talk to you about your ideas and who take an interest in your success. Regardless of whether or not you save a dime in taxes, you will certainly have a better understanding of what for most Americans is our single largest expense: Taxes.

Overview

"I'm proud to be paying taxes in America. But I could be just as proud for half the money."

—Arthur Godfrey

An Innovative Guide

In the United States, every year brings a new barrage of federally mandated tax laws. *Tax-Wise Business Ownership* is a fresh look at the ever-changing tax challenges that business owners face. It is a guide to business tax deductions and, most importantly, it provides innovative business tax-oriented strategies for accumulating and protecting personal and family wealth. However, this book is not the definitive answer to all business tax issues compiled by an almighty "tax-guru" / "master accountant," if such a person actually exists.

Tax-Wise Business Ownership was written by a businessman / lawyer to provide an understandable and user-friendly tool for fellow business owners and their professional advisors.

Tax-Wise Business Ownership gives a "big picture" of the taxation issues facing owners of businesses. With it, the experienced or the new business owner will be able to:

☐ Navigate through the complex federal tax matrix

☐ Identify areas to be discussed with professional advisors

☐ Detour around taxation danger zones

Scope

In order to build substantial financial security, it is essential to find the best ways to protect personal income from taxes. That's as true today as ever—whether your financial goals are in the hundreds, thousands, or millions. The techniques in this book range from fundamental strategies for finding business-related deductions to the tax-wise extraction of multimillion-dollar income from a business.

Whether your business is a full-time occupation or a sideline activity that is organized and conducted as a business, it may be possible to dramatically increase after-tax income. The key is to select the best tax-wise business structure while simultaneously optimizing all allowable business tax deductions.

Each year there are renewed efforts to crackdown on tax loopholes, even at times when legislators are handing out rebates and establishing lower federal tax rates. Therefore it is vitally important for the business owner to "zero in" on those strategies that remain viable tax-savers, while avoiding practices that are either on the regulator's "watch list" or no longer allowed.

Don't Go It Alone

The success of every tax-wise business and estate building technique depends upon personalizing it for each situation.

That customization takes teamwork between a knowledgeable, informed business owner and competent, professional advisors.

This book is a guide, but truly tax-wise business owners will always seek and utilize professional legal and financial advice. Remember, there is no single business tax strategy that will fit every situation and every individual. The bottom line—you must work closely with trusted and competent, professional advisors.

How This Book Is Organized

Topics are purposely presented in a manner that will be of interest to a wide spectrum of readers—from those planning a startup business to those running an established business. It is assumed that most readers have a basic understanding of the US tax system and principles of business operations and management.

The book starts with the very basics—the personal and psychological aspects of taxation. Although most writers avoid discussing this internalization, I believe that business owners must come to grips with psychological barriers in order to implement key techniques that will lead to *Tax-Wise Business Ownership.*

Whether you are a seasoned entrepreneur, business leader, or a neophyte starting a new venture, you need the basics before you can understand the strategies. The chapters of this book use a building-block approach that will help you increase your understanding of business taxation, and in particular, tax deductions.

Unfortunately, business deductions were not created equally—primarily because "doing business," from a tax standpoint, has more to do with form than with commercial substance. Here is where the complex matrix of business organizational structures must be understood before tax-wise business strategies can be introduced.

Under the governing laws of most states, there are seven general organizational structures ("forms") for conducting business:

- ☐ Sole Proprietorship
- ☐ General Partnership
- ☐ Limited Partnership
- ☐ C Corporation
- ☐ S Corporation
- ☐ Limited Liability Company
- ☐ Joint Venture

Each of these business forms has a very specific, complex, and unique set of federal income and expense recognition rules and associated taxes. Since the scope of this book is ultimately the accumulation and protection of personal and family wealth, the focus is on the business owner's personal tax issues as they filter through these business organizational structures.

Some of you probably own established businesses and therefore believe that reviewing other forms of doing business is superfluous. You are very wrong! As you will see in later chapters of this book, the business form is often the most critical tax-wise element necessary for success. Restructuring a business and/or using other forms of organization for particular endeavors may be a small tax-wise price to pay for owners to reach their ultimate goal of building substantial personal and family wealth.

Chapter Structure

Each chapter of this book begins with an explanation of the concepts to be covered, tax code references, governing laws, case studies, and/or private letter rulings—and concludes with endnote citations.

Examples

Tax-wise business techniques and their personal estate building benefits are noted throughout this book. When citing tax liabilities, the examples are calculated for the 2015 tax year, unless noted otherwise.

Tax Laws

Nothing seems to change faster than the rules and regulations for federal taxation. Before restructuring business activities or implementing any major tax strategy, business owners and tax advisors should always assure themselves that cited rulings and decisions have not been superseded (in whole or in part) since the date of this publication.

Private Letter Rulings

The Internal Revenue Service (IRS) publishes *private* letter rulings issued at the request of unidentified taxpayers. Although letter rulings may have been cited in the discussion of specific techniques, actions, or recommendations in this book, these rulings can only be relied upon by their recipients. Private letter rulings do not establish a precedent and do not carry the official status of a published revenue ruling.

Point of Emphasis

In order to highlight important information that warrants attention, the encompassing paragraph is preceded by the following symbol:

☑

Treatment

This book covers the subject matter in a general manner. It is not intended to fill the specific need of individual business owners. For example, each owner must determine the structure of his/her business, the plan for building his/her financial estate, and most importantly, how that structure and plan will be implemented.

Many factors bear on these determinations. Therefore, prospective and current business owners should review their individual situations with their attorney, accountant, estate planner, or other professional advisors. This consultation is especially important when dealing with tax laws because local and state legislation may adversely affect the outcome of business and estate-planning transactions that might otherwise be successful under federal rules and regulations.

Although we believe that *Tax-Wise Business Ownership* provides accurate and authoritative information on applicable tax rules that were in effect at the time of publication, readers should understand that this book is not intended to represent the rendering of legal, accounting, or other professional services. Readers who require such services or other expert assistance should consult competent professional advisors.

The Challenge

> *"Whoever admits that he is too busy to improve his methods has acknowledged himself to be at the end of his rope. And that is always the saddest predicament which anyone can get into."*
>
> —J. Ogden Armour

It has been my experience that people tend to shy away from and even fear things that they do not understand. Thus it is no surprise to me that most of the people I deal with completely ignore financial planning—whether it is simple estate planning or more complex tax reduction strategies. Business owners also often avoid the unknown, not realizing that they have powerful options available through their businesses to accumulate and protect personal and family wealth.

If readers get nothing else out of this book other than a basic under-standing of tax-wise business practices, I will consider my job as an author a success. However, for those readers who take the extra step and *utilize* the information, techniques, and strategies in *Tax-Wise Business Ownership*, this success is truly theirs. They will have taken an active role in creating financial security and will be on a very rewarding journey—both financially and intellectually.

CHAPTER

The Basics

"The hardest thing in the world to understand is the income tax."

—Albert Einstein

Relax

The most important thing you can do when it comes to taxes is relax. That advice is easy to give, but with images of mounds of paperwork, piles of receipts, complex rules and regulations, weeks of labor to fill out unintelligible forms, the risk of making mistakes, the threat of audits, the burdens of defending your actions, and the potential of large financial penalties—relaxing may seem impossible.

Stop and get a gut reaction to the word "tax." What does the word do to you? If you are like most people the reaction is anything but positive. The fact of the matter is that most people share a common emotion that cripples them from taking meaningful steps toward improving their financial situation. That emotion is fear. The good news is that it can be dispelled through knowledge. The truth is that knowledge without action will still leave you financially crippled, albeit much less fearful.

Because the federal tax system has become such a fear factory, most people do not push the system in order to exercise their right to pay the least amount that they may owe. Rather, they let the threat of audits and possibilities of penalties paralyze them with fear. The result: They err on the side of caution, seek to fit their deductions within hypothetically acceptable ranges, and/or immediately pay the most they could possibly owe.

Does any part of this discussion sound familiar? Unfortunately, it probably does. So what should you do? Relax. Absorb the information in this book. If you do, you will be on the path to becoming a tax-wise business owner. Knowledge and action are the cornerstones to overcoming fear.

Communicate

How often have you returned from a meeting with an attorney, accountant, financial advisor, or other professional and realized that if you had known the right questions to ask you would have been able to get the right answers? If you don't know the questions or can't steer the conversation toward the areas that are most important to you—it is unlikely that anyone will be able to give you valid answers. This failure to communicate is especially damaging in the business taxation and wealth-building arenas.

Outside professional advisors (attorneys, accountants, financial planners, etc.) are hired to advise and to work for you. Ordinarily they are not hired to direct business operations and personal activities. While it is one thing for an owner to know what he wants to accomplish in business, it is often quite another for him to have any idea of how to accomplish his goals in a tax-wise manner. And it is impossible to communicate desires to professionals and understand their recommendations without knowledge. This, coupled with the fact that most people will avoid unfamiliar subjects, may lead a business owner to opt for inaction—a decision which may result in paying significantly higher taxes than required, while severely limiting financial gains. The other extreme is a complete reliance on advisors to make critical business decisions, rather than learning about tax-wise techniques that are necessary to manage the business and maximize its potential.

☑ Saving money on taxes does not come from finding tax loopholes, using magic smoke and mirror schemes, or resorting to cheating on tax returns. It is the direct result of acquiring specific business-tax knowledge and using whatever is currently available under existing laws to your fullest advantage.

The US Tax System

"If Thomas Jefferson thought taxation without representation was bad, he should see how it is with representation."

—RUSH LIMBAUGH

The IRC

☑ This book addresses tax-wise business strategies that are allowed under the Internal Revenue Code (IRC or the Code), codified in title 26 of the United States Code. The IRC is concerned exclusively with *federal* taxes. While most states allow the same tax deductions as the IRC, it is important to note that there may be deductions that are not allowed in certain states. Or, vice versa, your state may allow generous deductions that are not available for federal tax filing under the IRS. These differences are beyond the scope of this book. For this reason, it is always advisable to hire a good accountant or other tax professional to assist you with the preparation of your taxes.

The tax laws of the IRC are in a constant state of modification. New legislation generally begins in the Ways and Means Committee of the House of Representatives. Like most laws, they are created through a sequence of committee meetings with testimony by third-party experts on specific tax matters, and then drafted into bills. The House Ways and Means Committee will typically work with other congressional committees that also have taxing authority as well as the Treasury Department on the drafting of each bill. Eventually, bills go to the House, where, if approved, they are forwarded to the Senate to undergo more committee meetings and debates before being sent to the floor of the Senate for approval. Finally, if the Senate approves a bill, the approved version will be sent to a new committee (a so-called "conference committee") that will draft the final version using the House and Senate's approved versions. The House and Senate must then approve the final version before it is sent to the

President to be vetoed or approved. If signed by the President, the bill becomes law and is added to the IRC.

When you hear about tax relief acts, new deductions, and changes in tax rates, you are really hearing about new laws being proposed or enacted. If the IRC does not cover an issue, then the only other controlling guidance is case law. Some accountants rely on regulations and private letter rulings, but ultimately it is the IRC and case law that dictate taxes.

The IRS

The Treasury Department administers the Internal Revenue Code ("IRC"). It, in turn, delegates the administrative support of the IRC to the Internal Revenue Service.

The IRS is nothing more than an enforcement (policing) agency that has been assigned the task of collecting taxes due under the IRC. The IRS does not participate in the proposal or drafting of the tax code. Writing the tax laws is left entirely up to Congress. Like your local policeman, the IRS exists to enforce the laws. However, policemen are thought of as public servants that seek a caring and protective relationship with the citizenry. The IRS on the other hand, is perceived as an iron-fisted agency that will destroy your life without a second thought if it thinks you have done something wrong. Few if any of its operational practices lead anyone to a contrary opinion.

Whatever your personal opinion of the IRS is, do not lose sight of the fact that the IRS ostensibly exists for our communal benefit. However nice that sounds, relationships with the IRS are no different than those with your local police—follow the laws and stay out of their way. The best strategy is to keep from doing things that cause you to pop up on their radar. This almost guarantees that you will not have problems with either.

On a Personal Level

The US tax system operates on a self-assessed basis in that each taxpayer computes the amount he or she owes and then automatically becomes liable for payment. The IRS reviews a small percentage of tax returns each year in order to make sure that taxpayers are paying the correct amount. On its face, this system appears to be a very reasonable and rational way for citizens to support their government. However, that view has been severely compromised because of the stories that taxpayers have heard about IRS abuses of power.

Probably the biggest reason that US citizens have developed a jaded attitude about the IRS is that agents are not in the habit of telling taxpayers when there is an overpayment of taxes. In addition, the IRS does not make it a practice to tell anyone about tax deductions that may have been overlooked. As a result, some may suspect that the IRS is an active proponent of maintaining the complexity of the US tax system—whereby the IRS can maintain:

- ☐ An unwarranted advantage in interpreting tax law
- ☐ Abusive enforcement and collection powers
- ☐ Job security

Responsibility

The responsibility to avoid overpayment of taxes, capture all of the deductions possible, and otherwise navigate the complex nuances of the tax laws are up to each taxpayer and his team of advisors. While this team approach may sound nice, only the business owner knows the details of the business and fully appreciates his personal financial position. And, it is highly unlikely that tax professionals will have any reasons to care more about business owners than themselves.

Taxpayers find themselves in a situation that is similar to a coach of a sports team. Every business owner needs to understand the dynamics of taxation, the skills and talents of each advisor, and the strengths and weakness of a proposed tax strategy before he or she can make a tax-wise decision about any proposal by the "team."

☑ It would be nice if each of us could completely abrogate tax decisions to others—but we can't. Ultimately the business owner is responsible. He must pay the taxes as well as the fees and penalties for all errors, not to mention the expenses that advisors pile up.

Collection, Collection, Collection

> *"We should be grateful we don't get all the government we pay for."*
> —Will Rogers

The US tax system is the juggernaut of all revenue generators. Income tax revenues alone exceed $3 *trillion* annually.[1] This amount does not include social security taxes; taxes on fuel,

Table 6. Gross Collections, by Type of Tax, Fiscal Years 1960–2014

[Money amounts are in thousands of dollars]

Fiscal year	Total Internal Revenue collections [1]	Total	Income taxes Business income taxes [2]	Income taxes Individual income tax [3]	Income taxes Estate and trust income tax [3]	Employment taxes [4]	Estate tax	Gift tax	Excise taxes [5]
	(1)	(2)	(3)	(4)	(5)	(6)	(7)	(8)	(9)
1960	91,774,803	67,125,126	22,179,414	44,945,711	n.a.	11,158,589	1,439,259	187,089	11,864,741
1961	94,401,086	67,917,941	21,764,940	46,153,001	n.a.	12,502,451	1,745,480	170,912	12,064,302
1962	99,440,839	71,945,305	21,295,711	50,649,594	n.a.	12,708,171	1,796,227	238,960	12,752,176
1963	105,925,395	75,323,714	22,336,134	52,987,581	n.a.	15,004,486	1,971,614	215,843	13,409,737
1964	112,260,257	78,891,218	24,300,863	54,590,354	n.a.	17,002,504	2,110,992	305,312	13,950,232
1965	114,434,634	79,792,016	26,131,334	53,660,683	n.a.	17,104,306	2,454,332	291,201	14,792,779
1966	128,879,961	92,131,794	30,834,243	61,297,552	n.a.	20,256,133	2,646,968	446,954	13,398,112
1967	148,374,815	104,288,420	34,917,825	69,370,595	n.a.	26,958,241	2,728,580	285,826	14,113,748
1968	153,636,838	108,148,565	29,896,520	78,252,045	n.a.	28,085,898	2,710,254	371,725	14,320,396
1969	187,919,560	135,778,052	38,337,646	97,440,406	n.a.	33,068,657	3,136,691	393,373	15,542,787
1970	195,722,096	138,688,568	35,036,983	103,651,585	n.a.	37,449,188	3,241,321	438,755	15,904,264
1971	191,647,198	131,072,374	30,319,953	100,752,421	n.a.	39,918,690	3,352,641	431,642	16,871,851
1972	209,855,737	143,804,732	34,925,546	108,879,186	n.a.	43,714,001	5,126,522	363,447	16,847,036
1973	237,787,204	164,157,315	39,045,309	125,112,006	n.a.	52,081,709	4,338,924	636,938	16,572,318
1974	268,952,254	184,648,094	41,744,444	142,903,650	n.a.	62,093,632	4,659,825	440,849	17,109,853
1975	293,822,726	202,146,097	45,746,660	156,399,437	n.a.	70,140,809	4,312,657	375,421	16,847,741
1976	302,519,792	205,751,753	46,782,956	158,968,797	n.a.	74,202,853	4,875,735	431,730	17,257,720
1976 [6]	75,462,780	49,567,484	9,808,905	39,758,579	n.a.	19,892,041	1,367,935	117,312	4,518,008
1977	358,139,417	246,805,067	60,049,804	186,755,263	n.a.	86,076,316	5,649,460	1,775,866	17,832,707
1978	399,776,389	278,438,289	65,380,145	213,058,144	n.a.	97,291,653	5,242,080	139,419	18,664,949
1979	460,412,185	322,993,733	71,447,876	251,545,857	n.a.	112,849,874	5,344,176	174,899	19,049,504
1980	519,375,273	359,927,392	72,379,610	287,547,782	n.a.	128,330,480	6,282,247	216,134	24,619,021
1981	606,799,103	406,583,302	73,733,156	332,850,146	n.a.	152,885,816	6,694,641	215,745	40,419,598
1982	632,240,506	418,599,768	65,990,832	352,608,936	n.a.	168,717,936	8,035,335	108,038	36,779,428
1983	627,246,793	411,407,523	61,779,556	349,627,967	n.a.	173,847,854	6,077,202	148,675	35,765,538
1984	680,475,229	437,071,049	74,179,370	362,891,679	n.a.	199,210,028	6,024,985	151,682	38,017,486
1985	742,871,541	474,072,327	77,412,769	396,659,558	n.a.	225,214,568	6,303,418	276,284	37,004,944
1986	782,251,812	497,406,391	80,441,620	416,964,771	n.a.	243,978,380	6,814,417	380,538	33,672,086
1987	886,290,590	568,311,471	102,858,985	465,452,486	n.a.	277,000,469	7,164,681	502,989	33,310,980
1988	935,106,594	583,349,120	109,682,554	473,666,566	n.a.	318,038,990	7,348,679	435,766	25,934,040
1989	1,013,322,133	632,746,069	117,014,564	515,731,504	n.a.	345,625,586	8,143,689	829,457	25,977,333
1990	1,056,365,652	650,244,947	110,016,539	540,228,408	n.a.	367,219,321	9,633,736	2,128,202	27,139,445
1991	1,086,851,401	660,475,445	113,598,569	546,876,876	n.a.	384,451,220	10,237,247	1,235,894	30,451,596
1992	1,120,799,558	675,673,952	117,950,796	557,723,156	n.a.	400,080,904	10,411,450	1,067,666	33,565,587
1993	1,176,685,625	717,321,668	131,547,509	585,774,159	n.a.	411,510,516	11,433,495	1,457,470	34,962,476
1994	1,276,466,776	774,023,837	154,204,684	619,819,153	n.a.	443,831,352	13,500,126	2,106,667	43,004,794
1995	1,375,731,835	850,201,510	174,422,173	675,779,337	n.a.	465,405,305	13,326,051	1,818,343	44,980,627
1996	1,486,546,674	934,368,068	189,054,791	745,313,276	n.a.	492,365,178	15,350,591	2,241,226	42,221,611
1997	1,623,272,071	1,029,513,216	204,492,336	825,020,880	n.a.	528,596,833	17,595,484	2,760,917	44,805,621
1998	1,769,408,739	1,141,335,868	213,270,011	928,065,857	n.a.	557,799,193	21,314,933	3,316,029	45,642,716
1999	1,904,151,888	1,218,510,654	216,324,889	1,002,185,765	n.a.	598,669,865	23,627,320	4,758,287	58,585,763
2000	2,096,916,925	1,372,732,596	235,654,894	1,137,077,702	n.a.	639,651,814	25,618,377	4,103,243	54,810,895
2001	2,128,831,182	1,364,941,523	186,731,643	1,178,209,880	n.a.	682,222,095	28,289,863	3,958,253	52,418,848
2002	2,016,627,269	1,249,171,681	211,437,773	1,037,733,908	n.a.	688,077,238	25,532,186	1,709,329	52,136,835
2003	1,952,929,045	1,181,355,176	194,146,298	987,208,878	n.a.	695,975,801	20,887,883	1,939,025	52,771,160
2004	2,018,502,103	1,220,868,119	230,619,359	990,248,760	n.a.	717,247,296	24,130,143	1,449,319	54,807,225
2005	2,268,895,122	1,414,595,831	307,094,837	1,107,500,994	n.a.	771,441,662	23,565,164	2,040,367	57,252,098
2006	2,518,680,230	1,617,183,944	380,924,573	1,236,259,371	n.a.	814,819,218	26,717,493	1,970,032	57,989,543
2007	2,691,537,557	1,761,777,263	395,535,825	1,366,241,437	n.a.	849,732,729	24,557,815	2,420,138	53,049,612
2008	2,745,035,410	1,780,306,008	354,315,825	1,400,405,178	25,585,005	883,197,626	26,543,433	3,280,502	51,707,840
2009	2,345,337,177	1,415,864,347	225,481,588	1,175,421,788	14,960,969	858,163,864	21,583,131	3,094,191	46,631,646
2010	2,345,055,978	1,453,926,748	277,937,220	1,163,687,589	12,301,939	824,188,337	16,930,741	2,820,095	47,190,057
2011	2,414,952,112	1,589,030,349	242,848,122	1,331,160,469	15,021,758	767,504,822	[7] 2,506,991	6,572,384	49,337,563
2012	2,524,320,134	1,669,298,095	281,461,580	1,371,402,290	16,434,225	784,396,853	12,340,655	2,109,594	56,174,937
2013	2,855,059,420	1,876,348,448	311,993,954	1,539,658,421	24,696,073	897,847,151	14,051,771	5,778,377	61,033,674
2014	3,064,301,358	1,996,765,080	353,141,112	1,614,213,171	29,410,796	976,223,247	17,572,338	[8] 2,582,617	71,158,076

n.a.—Not available. See footnote 3 below.

[1] Beginning with Fiscal Year 2009, excludes refunds credited to taxpayer accounts for tax liability in a subsequent year.

[2] Includes taxes on corporation income (Form 1120 series) and on unrelated business income from tax-exempt organizations (Form 990–T).

[3] Income tax reported for estates and trusts is included in individual income tax in Fiscal Years 1960–2007. Beginning with Fiscal Year 2008, estate and trust income tax is reported separately.

[4] Includes taxes for Old-Age, Survivors, Disability, and Hospital Insurance (OASDHI); unemployment insurance under the Federal Unemployment Tax Act (FUTA); and railroad retirement under the Railroad Retirement Tax Act (RRTA).

[5] Excludes excise taxes collected by the U.S. Customs and Border Protection and the Alcohol and Tobacco Tax and Trade Bureau. The Internal Revenue Service collected taxes on alcohol and tobacco until Fiscal Year 1988, and taxes on firearms until Fiscal Year 1991.

[6] Represents fiscal-year transitional period, July 1976 through September 1976, resulting from redefinition of the term "fiscal year." Fiscal Year 1976 covered July 1975 through June 1976 (earlier years were similarly defined). Fiscal Year 1977 covered October 1976 through September 1977 (subsequent years are similarly defined).

[7] The estate tax was temporarily repealed for deaths in Calendar Year 2010 before being reinstated retroactively with a $5-million exemption as part of the Tax Relief, Unemployment Insurance Reauthorization, and Job Creation Act of 2010. As a result of this legislation, the estates of 2010 decedents could elect to file either Form 706 (estate and generation-skipping transfer tax return), due September 19, 2011, or Form 8939 (allocation of increase in basis for property acquired from a decedent), due January 17, 2012. The law also provided a $5-million exemption for the estates of 2011 decedents. These tax law changes significantly reduced estate tax gross collections in Fiscal Year 2011 relative to other fiscal years.

[8] The amount of gift tax collections decreased from $5,778,377,000 in Fiscal Year (FY) 2013 to $2,582,617,000 in FY 2014. The Tax Relief, Unemployment Insurance Reauthorization, and Job Creation Act of 2010 raised the unified estate and gift tax credit to $5 million until December 31, 2012, after which the gift tax credit was to return to $1 million. Uncertainty over whether Congress would extend the higher credit led to a surge in gifts during early FY 2013. The $5 million exemption was made permanent on December 31, 2012, and indexed for inflation, as part of the American Taxpayer Relief Act of 2012 and as a result, the amount of gift tax reported in FY 2014 is more in line with historic trends.

NOTES:

Detail may not add to totals because of rounding.

All money amounts are in current dollars.

Partnership, S corporation, regulated investment company, and real estate investment trust data are not shown in this table since these entities generally do not have a tax liability. Instead, they pass any profits or losses to the underlying owners who include these profits or losses on their income tax returns.

This table shows gross collections. Gross collections less refunds equals net collections. See Table 1 for data on refunds and net collections.

SOURCE: Chief Financial Officer, Financial Management.

alcohol, tobacco, luxury items, firearms, and imports; estate and gift taxes; or state, city and county taxes. Estimates show that for every dollar US citizens earn, over 80 cents will end up somewhere in the federal tax system. The infamous "tax day" (the day that the average taxpayer has earned enough to pay his entire annual income tax bill) gets later and later each year. In fact, for most Americans, the IRS is their biggest creditor.

Staying Off the Radar Screen

Perhaps the most overlooked tax strategy is positioning financial affairs in such a way as to lower your chances of an audit. Obviously, if you paid the maximum tax obligation under the laws, your chance of audit may remain somewhat low. However, you can actually *lower* your risk of audit by employing certain tax strategies.

For example:

Assume that you are an individual who files a "plain vanilla" 1040 tax return each year with W-2 income of $50,000 and other income from various dealings of $55,000. Even if you do not attempt to receive deductions via schedule C, your audit risk would be 0.3%.[2] If you did file a schedule C, your audit risk jumps to 2.4%.[3]

If you had earned the extra $55,000 in a corporation or partnership, the audit rate on the extra income would have ranged between 0.4% and 0.9% and *lowered* the individual audit rate to 0.3% for an aggregate audit rate of 0.7% to 1.2%.[4] With a simple corporate or partnership structure, a taxpayer can receive numerous tax benefits that reduce taxes and build financial wealth along with the added benefit of reducing the risk of being audited.

Most taxpayers probably assume that if they use a formal business structure to receive portions of their income that this will increase their audit risk. However, for most of us, the opposite is true. Why? For the simple reason that businesses receive preferential treatment under the tax code. Perhaps the most telling statistic from the IRS is the "no change percent" or the percentages of returns that are scrutinized yet undergo no changes. Not surprisingly, the no change percent for formal business structures is more than double that of individuals.[5] Succinctly, the IRS has had more success recovering revenue when it audits individuals' returns than when it reviews business entity returns. Therefore, the IRS has more of an economic incentive to pursue individuals. In addition, most individuals are not represented by tax professionals who have the skill and training to challenge the IRS on interpretative issues of the IRC.

Considering the foregoing, it should not be a surprise to learn that formal businesses account for approximately 12% of the total taxes collected by the federal government.[6] The other 88% of tax revenue come from individuals, estates, and trusts. No wonder the IRS likes to scare us. We tend to overpay.

Keeping in mind that the IRS is essentially a business, it tends to scrutinize large corporations with earnings in excess of $250 million far more often than smaller corporations with earnings of $50,000. The utilization of a small formal business structure creates a scenario similar to a small fish swimming in an ocean filled with whales. The IRS has bigger fish to fry. Once again, you stay far below the IRS's radar.

Complexity Brings Opportunity

> *"The only thing that hurts more than paying an income tax is not having to pay an income tax."*
>
> —Lord Thomas Robert Dewar

As we all know, the federal tax system is unnecessarily complicated. Congress continually spews out new laws and codes concerning taxes. Every time there is a new effort at tax reform, the laws seem to become even more complicated. The Code alone is more than tens of thousands of pages. Because it is so complicated, taxpayers are often subjected to random interpretations by low-level IRS agents, or forced to look to regulations, private letter rulings, and tax courts for guidance. Not surprisingly, the volumes dedicated to interpreting the Code far exceed 1 million pages of text. In other words, the US tax law is an endless abyss of text that no one, and I mean no one, really comprehends.

This complexity may frighten most people, but tax-wise individuals view it as an advantage. They recognize that the IRS must navigate within the same convoluted, regulatory mess. The advantage goes to those citizens who:

- ☐ Have knowledge of specific sections of the Code that affect them
- ☐ Creatively apply the Code in the most tax-savvy manner

The fact that the laws governing taxation are so extensive and subject to interpretation means that an IRS agent cannot know all of the laws as well as all of the intervening court rulings. Additionally, many IRS employees receive their entire tax training via a six-week course. As a result, the IRS too often tumbles into the tax abyss. Therefore, it comes as no surprise that the IRS tends to target specific areas for its audits (i.e., home office deductions), rather than judge the veracity of each tax return.

Code of Conduct Relief

Changes in the laws governing the IRS and its collection practices have made significant strides toward providing sizeable tax relief. Gone are the days when IRS agents could act with impunity and without fear of recourse. Now the IRS is just like any other business in that it has to act responsibly, operate within a budget, and treat clients (taxpayers) fairly. If it fails to conduct itself in this manner, there are now laws in place that allow taxpayers to seek recourse against the IRS for improper conduct by its agents. Because of these rules, the IRS can no longer arbitrarily increase the frequency and intensity of taxpayer audits because (i) such practices are prohibited and (ii) they are not economically justifiable. Thus, there has been a dramatic reduction in the number of audits, and the IRS has shifted its focus to concentrate on areas that have the highest potential to recover the most tax revenue.

Income and Expenses

> *"The income tax has made more liars out of the American people than golf has. Even when you make a tax form out*

> *on the level, you don't know when it's through, if you are a crook or a martyr."*
>
> —WILL ROGERS

Qualified tax professionals focus on both the income and expenses of their clients when developing tax-wise strategies.

For example:

> If a taxpayer can transfer an income producing activity into a tax-deferred entity (such as a retirement plan), while simultaneously making that transfer (contribution) a deductible expense, that income is eliminated for tax calculation purposes. In addition, additional income from the transferred activity will compound without taxes in future years. Eventually, income taxes will have to be paid as retirement distributions to the taxpayer, but the amount amassed (after-tax) will far exceed other tax-burdened alternatives. This transfer and deduction approach utilizes both income-limiting and expense-offset strategies.

Chapter 5 is devoted to business expenses that can, under certain circumstances, be deductible. The ultimate tax liability solution is to offset as much business and personal income as possible by authorized expense deductions. Aside from being deductible, the *degree* to which the expense is deductible is very important. The goal is to have the entire expense be 100% deductible, without being subject to any offsetting limitations imposed by income, etc.

For example:

It is almost impossible to receive any tangible tax benefits by offsetting medical expenses as an itemized expense using tax form 1040. This is due to the fact that only the portion of the medical expenses incurred in that tax year that exceed 7.5% of the adjusted gross income of the taxpayer (the "floor") are allowed as an offset (deduction) against income.

Dollar-for-Dollar Deductions

When a dollar of income is offset by a dollar deduction, the net taxable income is zero. There is no federal income tax. This is called a "dollar-for-dollar" deduction. The taxpayer is allowed to offset income by the expense at a degree of 100%. This is the tax-wise goal.

To achieve this goal, business owners must understand the various business structures and the ramifications that these structures have on taxes. (See Chapter 3.)

When in Doubt, Deduct

☑ If you are comfortable that you are within the interpretive bounds of current tax laws, then go for the deduction! First of all, the chances of being audited are probably less than 1%. Secondly, if you have a sound, arguable position, but the IRS takes a different view, you may be able to negotiate a favorable settlement. If your comfort level only allows you to take a partial deduction, then, in the unlikely event that you are audited, you have a card to play. Wouldn't it be nice to say to the auditor, "Thanks for the audit, you made me realize that I missed taking this major deduction . . . ." If, on the other hand, you are concerned that a deduction will trigger an audit, then it may not be worth the risk. Either way, it is nice to have the option.

The key to being successful with your tax reduction strategies is going in with your eyes open. You want to know which deductions are questionable and which ones are not. This helps you assess the risks, and it should allow you sleep better at night—since you will be making decisions that are within your comfort zone.

Keep in mind that tax strategies benefit you. Nobody else— just you and your family benefit. This is one of the few times where every minute you spend goes to your bottom line, rather than to that of someone else. For whatever reason, Americans seem to feel uncomfortable—almost guilty—about improving their own financial position. If you follow the strategies contained in this book, your conscience will remain clean.

Audits

"In seeking honey expect the sting of bees."

—**Arabian proverb**

☑ Audits are an inevitable part of the US tax system. There are no rules or magic guidelines that will guarantee that your return will not be picked for an audit. Fortunately, there are steps you can take to get through an audit that will minimize stress and maximize your chances of keeping your tax deductions and tax-wise strategies intact.

Audit Period

The IRS generally has three years from the date the return was due or the date it was filed, whichever date is later, in which to audit your return. There are important exceptions. If the taxpayer's omission is more than 25% of gross income, the audit period is extended to six years. And, a return may be audited at any time if it was prepared and filed under fraudulent circumstances.

Record Keeping

It is vital that you keep records to substantiate and support the items of income and deductions that you claimed. In the event that your tax return is audited, you will be glad you thought ahead and retained your records. These records should include the following: tax returns (both business and personal); all permanent business records; proof of tax payments; documents that establish basis of investment, inherited, and gifted property; stock investment records; and documents explaining all personal financial transactions (e.g., bills of sale, invoices, receipts, canceled checks, etc.). Refer to the appendixes at the end of this book for an outline of the required time frames for keeping your various records.

Audit Representation

☑ After the initial shock of receiving an audit notice from the IRS has subsided, one of the first questions you will ask yourself is, "Do I require, or should I have, professional representation?" Unfortunately there is no hard-and-fast answer, but here are a few guidelines that may help you decide one way or the other:

- ☐ When you receive notice, call to find out what the audit will cover. For example, you might believe that all that the IRS really wants is for you to provide a receipt or canceled check that will substantiate a deduction that you claimed. In this case, you might want to handle the audit yourself since it doesn't appear to be very complex. If, on the other hand, more complicated issues might be involved—you would want to be represented by a professional advisor.
- ☐ Know yourself before you decide to be your own representative. Take a long hard look at your personality, the image that you project to others, and the way that you handle confrontations. You must candidly weight your ability to remain civil when under a barrage of questions that may appear to attack your veracity. Will you become antagonistic? If so, regardless of the simplicity of the audit, you need professional representation. IRS agents are only human, if you "bark" at them, they may find ways to "bite" you hard in your pocketbook.
- ☐ If you are representing yourself (which I would almost never recommend), start the audit session by asking to see the IRS agent's credentials. This is vital because there are two classes of IRS agents and it makes a big difference which one is reviewing your tax return. If your reviewing agent is a "special agent," terminate the interview immediately and do not discuss any matter until you have sought legal counsel. Reason: special agents are concerned with matters of tax fraud.

On the other hand, "revenue agents" conduct normal examinations to determine if adjustment or reassessments are necessary. They are assigned the run-of-the-mill cases.

- ☐ Even if you do start out representing yourself, things may get out of hand. Then what? If you sense that you cannot successfully communicate with the agent and/or things are taking a nasty turn for the worse, ask to adjourn the audit immediately. This will give you time to seek professional advice.

- ☐ The playing field is leveled when a professional represents a taxpayer in an audit. The situation is radically altered because neither the representative nor the IRS agent has a personal stake in the issues. The audit can be discussed on a professional level without the emotions that you might bring to the situation. As a result, it is usually better to be represented by an expert than to try to meet with the IRS on your own.

- ☐ Many representatives prefer to conduct business with the IRS without the taxpayer ever being present. This eliminates the risk of the client interrupting discussions or inadvertently blurting out damaging information under a false hope of being helpful. It also leaves the professional advisor with the ability to stop negotiations in order to seek the "higher authority" of the client's approval. In addition, the representative can more easily use "horse trading" to concede one area of contention in exchange for receiving concessions from the IRS on others. Remember, an IRS agent is always more likely to horse trade with a professional. That split-down-the-middle solution may be the key to a good settlement.

Selecting a Representative

☑ There are three basic categories of tax representatives to select from. All of them (except attorneys), have limits as to the extent that they can represent taxpayers before the IRS. Therefore, the selection of a representative most likely will depend on the types of problems that the audit might address.

- ☐ **Tax Attorneys** are at the top of the list. They can represent you at any stage—from the initial audit right through to the level of appellate courts.

- ☐ **Certified Public Accountants** (CPAs) are automatically licensed to appear before the IRS. However, when a case involves litigation, they are limited to appearances before the Tax Court. If the matter requires an appeal of a Tax Court ruling, you will need an attorney.

- ☐ **Enrolled Agents** are individuals that are licensed to practice before the IRS, and they may or may not be accountants. Enrolled Agents cannot represent clients beyond the level of an administrative appeal without passing a special exam specifically for Tax Court practice.

Protecting Yourself

☑ You will want to request that the agent clearly define the scope of the examination as early in the process as possible. This will allow you to supply only the records needed without giving the examiner a chance to browse through all of your files.

☑ Make an effort to be cooperative with the IRS agent, but don't go overboard. In general, you will get the audit over more quickly and with more favorable results if you fully cooperate with the examining agent. Lack of cooperation will slow the exam, and refusal to provide any document will raise suspicions. However, it is not necessary to provide more information than needed to answer a specific question.

☑ Between the time that the exam concludes and the completion of the agent's report, you may have a chance to discuss proposed adjustments and reach a disposition of your case. Reaching an agreement at the agent's level is an advantage because less evidence is required to establish a claim. IRS agents at this level are generally less experienced and may raise fewer issues. In addition, by ending the process at this point, you may be able to avoid further expense and personal anxiety. Acknowledging obvious errors promptly and providing the data necessary to recalculate your tax liabilities will often play in your favor. However, this does not necessarily hold true for areas in which your backup data is weak or where governing rules are open to interpretation.

☑ Upon completion of the exam, the IRS agent will prepare a report for his superiors, in summary form, including the reasons for adjustments to your taxes. He will ask you to sign a waiver agreeing to his revised assessment of taxes. Each signed report and waiver is sent up the chain for what is usually a routine approval. Signing of the waiver does not prohibit the IRS from reopening the case within the time period allowed for an audit. But, if you sign a waiver, you are prohibited from challenging the IRS assessment (contained within the report) through the Tax Court. Therefore, signing is advisable if the assessment is based on obvious return errors or the amount is insufficient to warrant further action on your part. However, you should not sign the waiver if you feel the agent seriously over assessed your errors, refused to adequately consider your position, or misinterpreted the law. If you do not sign the waiver, it will automatically trigger appellate or post-audit IRS procedures. And, you should hire a talented representative if you don't already have one by now.

Moving On

"Behind an able man there are always other able men."
—Chinese Proverb

The remainder of this book is comprised of tax strategies. Unlike the common phrase that you hear on many television shows—you are encouraged to try all of these strategies at home. Please read the pages with the following thought in mind: *You do not have to learn how to take all of the deductions, you only need to educate yourself so that you will be able to tell someone else to claim the deduction for you.* The likes of Forbes, Ford, and Gates have all learned the principles of maximizing their financial affairs by utilizing the skills of people around them.

Rather than dreaming of owning yachts and mansions, the most successful tax-wise business owners dream of finding the perfect team of accountants, attorneys, and financial professionals to run their affairs so that they can enjoy their yachts and nice homes. Ultimately, the concept that is most important is building a strong foundation under your financial affairs. There is no better foundation than a sound financial education plus an experienced, capable team of advisors.

Notes

1. The most recent statistics are available on-line at *www.irs.gov*. The annual Data Book (usually Publication 55B) contains statistics ranging from tax revenues collected to tax revenues collected per return audited.
2. The audit data used for the book was via the IRS yearly report was for 2014.
3. See endnote #1.
4. Audit rate for "C" corporations with total assets less than $250,000 – 0.4%; for "S" corporations – 0.40%; for partnerships – 0.4%; and for individuals (non-schedule C filers) earning $50,000 to $100,000 – 0.4%.
5. Under the example illustrated on the previous page, the "No Change Rate" for the individual scrutinized by a revenue agent would have been 5%, while the "C" corporation, "S" corporation and partnership's would have been 35%, 36%, and 44% respectively.
6. IRS Collections, "Table 6 – Internal Revenue Gross Collections, by Type of Tax, Fiscal Years 1960–2014."

CHAPTER

The Tax Foundation

"Business more than any other occupation is a continual dealing with the future; it is a continual calculation, an instinctive exercise in foresight."

—HENRY R. LUCE

Tax Planning

"The will to win is worthless if you do not have the will to prepare."

—THANE YOST

To become tax-wise, business owners must take full responsibility for the planning and execution of their tax saving strategies. More often than not, business owners confuse good tax planning with tax return preparation, which they leave to their accountants. They naively think that when a tax return is filed that their tax plan has been magically formulated and executed to perfection. This is akin to believing that filing for a business license will somehow in and of itself make a successful enterprise.

☑ Planning and implementing tax-wise business strategies are year-round jobs that cannot be done at tax filing time while looking back at last year's results. They demand proactive leadership and participation from the business owner—but these efforts will be richly rewarded if done properly. Remember, you have a choice. You can either work to reduce your federal and state income taxes, taxes on your retirement plans, and estate taxes—or you can allow the government to feast from the fruits of your labor. The choice is up to you. I guarantee that you will pay, and pay, and pay unless and until you successfully use the government's own tax laws to limit or completely eliminate taxes.

The Taxpayer

All discussions from here on will be based on the tax consequences for a cash basis taxpayer. A cash basis taxpayer is one who declares income and deductions "as the cash flows" either in or out, i.e., when salary is received, rather than when it is earned. This is the opposite of an accrual basis taxpayer who recognizes income and expenses as they are incurred.

Classifying Tax-Wise Strategies

All tax-wise strategies fall within one of the following classifications:

Tax-Wise Income Strategies
—those that control income recognition
Tax-Wise Expense Strategies
—those that control deductions from income

Rather than fight with the IRS, tax-wise business owners use tax laws to eliminate or to significantly reduce federal and state income, retirement, and estate taxes. The most effective results are obtained through a combination of income and expense strategies that are customized for the business owner's specific situation. However, before they can start to do this, business owners must learn the methods that are used in each of these tax-wise strategy classifications, as well as the IRS definitions that apply to each.

Tax-Wise Income Strategies

☑ There are four general methods that you can use to control your income in order to implement tax-wise strategies. You can:

- ☐ Decrease income—for example, transfer it to others
- ☐ Transform taxable into nontaxable income
- ☐ Defer income receipt into a future tax period
- ☐ Reclassify income from a tax standpoint

Definition of Income

Having a clear understanding of what the Code defines as income is very important to tax-wise business owners because the type of income dictates which losses and expenses can be used most effectively to reduce taxable income.

Under federal tax laws, "income" is defined as any acquisition of wealth, excluding gifts and inheritances. This is perceptibly different from the layman's concept of income, which is viewed as take-home pay that is derived solely from employment. In fact, the Supreme Court has ruled that:

> Income may be defined as the gain derived from capital, labor, or from both combined, provided it be understood to include profit gained through a sale or conversion of capital assets.[1]

Section 61 (§61) of the IRC defines "gross income" as:

> (a) . . . Except as otherwise provided in this subtitle, gross income means all income from whatever source derived, including (but not limited to) the following items:
>
>> Compensation for services, including fees, commissions, fringe benefits, and similar items;
>>
>> Gross income derived from business;
>>
>> Gains derived from dealings in property;
>>
>> Interest;
>>
>> Rents;
>>
>> Royalties;
>>
>> Dividends;
>>
>> Alimony and separate maintenance payments;

Annuities;

Income from life insurance and endowment contracts;

Pensions;

Income from discharge of indebtedness;

Distributive share of partnership gross income;

Income in respect of a decedent; and

Income from an interest in an estate or trust.

Income Exclusions

In essence, income includes all gains derived from labor or capital, except those specifically excluded by law. Some important areas of gain that are not considered as income are:

- ☐ Gifts and inheritances—nontaxable to the recipient
- ☐ Return of the original capital—such as amounts invested in a business or equity purchase
- ☐ Unrealized appreciation—the increase in value of appreciated investment property that has not been sold

Income Categories

The IRC further separates the types of income into categories that can be viewed as broadly identifying the activities that are used by taxpayers to produce them. Prior to 1986, the Code recognized two categories—"earned income" and "investment income." The Tax Reform Act of 1986 added a third category—"passive income."

> "Earned income" is compensation received by a taxpayer for personally providing goods or services to others. Social security tax is calculated and paid based on the taxpayer's earned income.

> "Investment income" is gain that is realized from investment portfolios. This category includes interest, dividends, royalties, annuity payments, and capital gains or losses from the sale of portfolio holdings.[2] The portion of investment income that is generated by long-term capital gains is taxed at a rate between 0% and 23.8% (at the highest bracket, inclusive of Net Investment Income Tax) in 2016, as opposed to the rate applied to the taxpayer's other taxable income, which stands at a top rate of 39.6%.

> "Passive income" is income from activities involving any trade or business in which the taxpayer is not directly and materially involved—so called "passive" activities.[3] This category includes income from any partnership, business, or other ownership interest where the taxpayer does not participate in management decisions. All rental activities are passive, regardless of the taxpayer's management or level of participation. Passive income is distinct and different from investment portfolio income.

☑ With the exception of investment income that is derived from long-term capital gains, the three categories of income are all taxed at the same rate. Therefore, distinguishing between these categories is not required to determine the taxability of this income. However, income must be categorized in order to determine the type of loss an activity may generate because the income category establishes the portion of an associated loss that can be deducted on a tax return.

Capital Gains and Losses

One of the most important taxation concepts is that of capital gains and losses. A capital gain or loss is the difference between the purchase price (basis) of a "capital asset" and the price received upon its sale (proceeds).

Under Section 1221(a) of the IRC,

> ... the term 'capital asset' means property held by the taxpayer (whether or not connected with his trade or business), but does not include:
>
> (1) stock in trade of the taxpayer or other property of a kind which would properly be included in the inventory of the taxpayer if on hand at the close of the taxable year, or property held by the taxpayer primarily for sale to customers in the ordinary course of his trade or business;
>
> (2) property, used in his trade or business, of a character which is subject to the allowance for depreciation provided in section 167, or real property used in his trade or business;

(3) a copyright, a literary, musical, or artistic composition, a letter or memorandum, or similar property, held by–

(A) a taxpayer whose personal efforts created such property,

(B) in the case of a letter, memorandum, or similar property, a taxpayer for whom such property was prepared or produced . . .

Investment securities and a taxpayer's personal property are considered capital assets.

The IRS uses the length of time that the taxpayer owned an interest in a capital asset (holding period) to determine whether a gain (or loss) is a long- or short-term capital gain (or loss). If the holding period is one year or less, the gain (or loss) is short-term—more than one year, it is long term.

All capital gains or losses are recognized, for tax purposes, in the tax year during which the capital asset was sold.

Capital losses offset capital gains, and any excess may be used by the taxpayer to offset up to $3,000 of ordinary annual income on a dollar-for-dollar basis. Capital losses above these limitations are accumulated and carried forward indefinitely until they are used to offset capital gains and ordinary income in future years.

All net short-term gains are added to ordinary income and taxed at the ordinary tax rate for the taxpayer's progressive rate tax bracket.

All net long-term gains are taxed at either 0%, 15%, or 20% for 2016, depending on the taxpayer's tax bracket.

Unlike the limitations imposed on claiming capital losses, there are no limits on the amount of net capital gains that are subject to federal taxes. If a taxpayer makes a capital gain, the federal government taxes the entire amount. On the other hand, any net capital loss in excess of the $3,000 limited offset against ordinary income must be carried forward to following years. By any measure, this is a double standard.

There are three exceptions where capital gains may be taxed at rates higher than 20%:

1. The taxable part of a gain from selling Section 1202 qualified small business stock is taxed at a maximum 28% rate.
2. Net capital gains from selling collectibles (such as coins or art) are taxed at a maximum 28% rate.
3. The portion of any un-recaptured Section 1250 gain from selling Section 1250 real property is taxed at a maximum 25% rate.

Passive Income and Losses

Except under restricted conditions in the area of passive real estate rental income, the Code limits deduction of losses from passive activities to the amount of the taxpayer's passive income. All excess passive losses are carried forward to following years and/or until the property is sold. However, once again, all of the net passive income is taxable in the year it is received.

Tax-Wise Expense Strategies

"The best way to save money is not to lose it."

—Les Willams

☑ There are four general expense methods that business owners can use to implement tax-wise strategies. They can:

- ☐ Increase deductible expenses by making nondeductible into deductible expenses;
- ☐ Transform them into a more favorable form—for example, from itemized personal deductions into business expenses;
- ☐ Accelerate their recognition into the current tax period;
- ☐ Create more deductions by reclassifying normal personal expenses.

Expenses Categories

The Code classifies each deduction claimed by taxpayers for an expense incurred during the tax year into one of two distinct categories: personal and business.

☑ The differences between these two expense categories is important because of how deductions are offset against income on a taxpayer's return or disallowed completely by the IRS. Obviously, the objective is to use one or all of the tax-wise expense methods in order to maximize allowable deductions (expenses). By further concentrating on the allowable deductions that can be used to offset income on a dollar-for-dollar basis, the tax-wise business owner will reach his ultimate tax-reduction goal.

In general, when personal expenses are allowed to be deducted, the Code limits the extent to which they can be used to offset income. More often than not, personal expenses are completely nondeductible. On the other hand, business expenses are generally fully deductible.[4] Therefore, one of the most effective tax-wise expense strategies is to claim a business deduction rather than a personal deduction if the expense meets the IRS tests as a qualified business expense.

> For example, if you go out to lunch to discuss business with a potential client, you have the option of keeping the expense as a personal expense (nondeductible) or a business expense (deductible). The choice is yours.

Undoubtedly, this example is very simplified—but I assure you that the IRS looks very keenly at what expenses can be deducted from income. They look at whether the expense is necessary, ordinary, and reasonable to generate the income—and allowed under the existing federal tax code. The next section examines this IRS expense test in more detail.

Definition of Business Expense

Section 162 of the Code governs most business expenses. There are provisions that spell out particular deductions (i.e., fringe benefits), but the vast majority of expenses are covered within this section.

§162. TRADE OR BUSINESS EXPENSES.

(a) IN GENERAL.

There shall be allowed as a deduction all the ordinary and necessary expenses paid or incurred during the taxable year in carrying on any trade or business, including–

(1) A reasonable allowance for salaries or other compensation for personal services actually rendered;

(2) Traveling expenses (including amounts expended for meals and lodging other than amounts which are lavish or extravagant under the circumstances) while away from home in the pursuit of a trade or business; and

(3) Rentals or other payments required to be made as a condition to the continued use or possession, for purposes of the trade or business, of property to which the taxpayer has not taken or is not taking title or in which he has no equity.

☑ The IRS test as to whether an expense is an allowable deduction against a specific source of income has four basic questions:

- ☐ Is the expense necessary to produce that income?
- ☐ Is the expense commonly encountered and ordinarily required for that type of business activity?
- ☐ Is the expense reasonable when measured against the amount of income generated?

☐ Is the expense legally allowed under existing federal tax statutes?

The answers to the questions about "necessary, ordinary, and reasonable" are clearly subjective. For example, an expense does not have to be indispensable to be considered "necessary." Because each tax return is unique, the answers to these questions will vary from taxpayer to taxpayer. This means that tax-wise business owners have wide latitude to interpret what constitutes "necessary, ordinary, and reasonable" expenses. However, business owners must know the Code because certain expenses are legally disallowed, regardless of how "necessary, ordinary, and reasonable" they might be for the business activities involved.

There are a few tax-wise strategies in this book that employ both personal and business deductions—but the majority focus exclusively on business. For more information on IRC §162 deductions, refer to Regulation 1.162-1. It lists many of the standard business deductions along with any restrictions that may apply. One note of caution, regulations are merely interpretations of the Code and your reading may differ significantly from that of the IRS.

The Power of Business Deductions

The creation of business deductions ultimately rests on your shoulders. How you handle your affairs has a tremendous impact on how much tax you will pay. For example, business owners may elect to expense certain otherwise depreciable business assets.

IRC, §179(a)

> A taxpayer may elect to treat the cost of any section 179 property as an expense which is not chargeable to capital account. Any cost so treated shall be allowed as a deduction for the taxable year in which the section 179 property is placed in service.

The net result is that a business owner can write off the purchase price of a broad range of assets required for his business as a deductible expense against his business income. But, if he fails to claim the business asset under Section 179, the business owner can only claim a fraction of its costs as depreciation in the year the asset was purchased.

The opportunity to use §179 to reduce taxes is very important, however, the Code limits the total value of the property that can be written off in any year to:

IRC, §179(b)

> (1) DOLLAR LIMITATION.
>
> The aggregate cost which may be taken into account under subsection (a) for any taxable year shall not exceed
>
> (A) $250,000 in the case of taxable years beginning after 2007 and before 2010,
>
> (B) $500,000 in the case of taxable years beginning in 2010, 2011, 2012, 2013, 2014,
>
> (C) $25,000 in the case of taxable years beginning after 2014.

(2) REDUCTION IN LIMITATION.

The limitation under paragraph (1) for any taxable year shall be reduced (but not below zero) by the amount by which the cost of section 179 property placed in service during such taxable year exceeds

(A) $800,000 in the case of taxable years beginning after 2007 and before 2010,

(B) $2,000,000 in the case of taxable years beginning in 2010, 2011, 2012, 2013, or 2014,

(C) $200,000 in the case of taxable years beginning after 2014.

The most important §179 limitation for small businesses is that the amount claimed cannot exceed the income derived from the business.

IRC, §179(b)

(2) LIMITATION BASED ON INCOME FROM TRADE OR BUSINESS.

(A) IN GENERAL.

The amount allowed as a deduction under subsection (a) for any taxable year (determined after the application of paragraphs (1) and (2)) shall not exceed the aggregate amount of taxable income of the taxpayer for such taxable year which is derived from the active conduct by the taxpayer of any trade or business during such taxable year.

Business Startup Example

Joe decides to start an underwater photography business as a sole proprietor. He purchases $4,000 of photographic equipment, obtains the required licenses, and converts one of the bedrooms in his home into an office. Joe continues to work as a foreman on the graveyard shift at a manufacturing plant where he earns $46,500 annually. Joe was in business by October but spent the remainder of the year taking underwater photos to finish his marketing portfolio, which cost him $1,000. By the end of the year Joe had no revenue but was very committed to the venture.

Scenario A

As the tax year closed, Joe asked a neighbor, Ima Fraid, for advice. Ima told Joe that the IRS might consider his photography business a hobby (rather than a business) and that the photographic equipment was really Joe's personal property. In addition, Ima Fraid cautioned Joe not to claim any business deductions when he filed his tax return. Using Ima Fraid's advice, Joe calculated that he had a net taxable income of $37,500, and, since he was single, Joe was in the 25% federal tax bracket and owed $5,911 in federal income tax plus 5% to the state ($1,725). In addition, Joe had 7.65% of his gross wages withheld for FICA ($3,022). He wasn't very pleased to realize that he would be out $10,658 to the government if he did nothing—nearly 29% of his entire gross income for the year.

Scenario B

Joe began to question the wisdom of Ima Fraid's counsel. He knew he was in business and thought he should get some professional advice. After a session with an accountant, Joe immediately sat down and recalculated his tax liabilities. Since Joe had no business income he could not claim a §179 expense deduction for the new photography equipment, but he could claim the portfolio development costs as business expense deductions. Joe lowered his taxable income to $33,500. He now was in the 15% tax bracket and owed the IRS $4,594 and the state $1,675. He still had paid $2,563 in FICA, but by simply converting personal (nondeductible) expenses into fully deductible business expenses, Joe saved $1,826—a nice bottom-line boost for his startup business. That lowered his taxes to $8,832—an 18% decrease in taxes paid. Not a bad start.

Scenario C

After Joe started his photography business he cut back his hours at the plant and his W-2 earnings dropped to $39,500. However, Joe was very happy that he was able to keep his gross income at $43,500 by completing several photography assignments that brought in $4,000. Again, Joe had 7.65% of his W-2 pay (now $39,500) withheld for FICA ($3,022), and he still had $9,000 in itemized deductions. The $4,000 in billings from the photography business was offset by a $4,000 §179 business expense deduction for the photography equipment. That, plus the $1,000 portfolio development business expense, reduced Joe's taxable income to $29,500. Joe owed the IRS $3,994 (15% bracket) and the state $1,475 (5%) for income taxes. He paid the government $8,491 out of a gross income of $43,500. Less than 20% going to taxes.

Tax Savings Comparison

By successfully converting personal deductions into business deductions *and* earned income into business income in Scenario C, Joe saved $2,167 more than Scenario A and $1,826 more than Scenario B in income taxes and FICA withholding.

The following three tables compare Joe's taxable income (Table 2), and tax plus FICA savings (Table 3) the three scenarios. (*Note*: These savings are on an annual basis.)

Table 2

Taxable Income Comparison

	Scenario			Comparisons		
	A	B	C	A to B	A to C	B to C
W-2 Income	$43,500	$43,500	$39,500	$0	$4,000	$4,000
Business Income	—	—	$4,000	—	$4,000	$4,000
Itemized Deductions	($9,000)	($9,000)	($9,000)	—	—	—
Business Deductions	—	($1,000)	($1,000)	($1,000)	($1,000)	—
§179 Deductions	—	—	($4,000)	—	($4,000)	($4,000)
Taxable Income	$34,500	$33,500	$29,500	$1,000	$5,000	$4,000
Federal Income Tax Bracket	25%	15%	15%	10%	10%	—

Table 3

Tax Plus FICA Savings Comparison

	Scenario			Comparisons		
	A	B	C	A to B	A to C	B to C
FICA (7.65%)	$3,022	$2,563	$3,022	—	$0	$765
Federal Income Tax	$5,911	$4,594	$3,994	$1,317	$1,917	$600
State Tax (5%)	$1,725	$1,675	$1,475	$100	$300	$200
Total Tax + FICA	$10,658	$8,832	$8,491	$1,826	$2,167	($341)

Equivalent Gross Income Comparison

The costly error of not making tax-wise business decisions shows up when we analyze Joe's pretax W-2 income. Joe would need to have the same net after-tax and FICA from all three scenarios.

For Scenario A, on every additional dollar of W-2 income he earned, Joe faced:

- ☐ 25% federal income tax bracket
- ☐ 5.0% state income tax
- ☐ 7.65% FICA withholding

This is a 37.65% tax and FICA burden. Therefore, for Joe to net $1.00 more after this burden, he would need to earn $1.60.

$$\$1.60 = \$1.00/(1-37.65\%)$$

Joe's gross income and cost of the photography equipment was the same in all three scenarios—$43,500 and $4,000. However, in comparison with Scenario A, Joe saved $1,826 in taxes in Scenario B, and he had a savings of $341 in reduced taxes and FICA withholding in Scenario C.

Table 5
Tax & FICA Burden Comparison

	Scenario			Comparisons	
	A	B	C	A to B	A to C
FICA Burden	7.65%	7.65%	7.65%	—	—
Federal Income Tax Bracket	25%	15%	15%	10%	10%
State Income Tax Rate	5.0%	5.0%	5.0%	—	—
Total Tax and FICA Burden	37.65%	27.65%	27.65%	10%	10%
W-2 Income Required to Net $1 After-tax & FICA	$1.60	$1.38	$1.38	$0.22	$0.22

Purchasing the Equipment Comparison

How much did Joe really pay for his new photography equipment in gross earnings?

Tax-wise business owners would offset the $4,000 of business income by a §179 business expense deduction as Joe did in Scenario C. For Joe, this was a dollar-for-dollar exchange and the most efficient use of his allowable §179 business expense deduction. Joe saw this clearly when he realized that in order to have $4,000 (after taxes and FICA withholding) for the photography equipment, he would need W-2 income of:

- ☐ $6,400 in Scenario A ($4,000 times 1.60)
- ☐ $5,520 in Scenario B ($4,000 times 1.38)

He also reasoned that he would have a very realistic way to compare the scenarios if he calculated the gross he would have to earn to:

- ☐ Purchase the photography equipment and
- ☐ Net the same dollars after business expenses, taxes, and FICA as he did in Scenario C.

Table 6
Gross Earnings Comparison

	Scenario		
	A	B	C
Gross earnings needed to purchase equipment	$6,400	$5,520	$4,000
Additional gross income required to equal Scenario C's net after-tax and FICA $s	$2,921	$554	—
Total gross earnings needed to buy equipment and have the same net $s	$9,321	$6,074	$4,000
Source of gross earnings	W-2	W-2	Business

Which is preferable?

- [ ] Earning $4,000 in gross business income

    or

- [ ] Earning $8,570 in W-2 wages

In this scenario, would Joe end up with the same amount after taxes and FICA? The tax-wise business choice for Joe is obvious.

Overcoming Your Reluctance

You may be asking yourself, "Why haven't I taken business deductions before?" Well, the answer to that question is generally one of two things. Either your accountant or tax professional told you that you would not qualify—or you simply did not know that you could qualify.

The plain and simple truth is that you really had no way to know. The fact is that financial literacy is rarely taught in our education system. To compound this problem, many of us (including accountants and tax professionals) have a fear of the unknown. Many advisors will automatically say you cannot deduct certain things because they are afraid on three fronts:

- [ ] Afraid of tangling with the IRS and being wrong
- [ ] Afraid of losing a client (ignorance is bliss)
- [ ] Afraid of being held professionally liable for a mistake

Fortunately, tax-wise business owners know that these fears are generally irrational. Truly tax-wise individuals realize that if they were to follow all of the conflicting advice, third-party interpretations, and isolated private rulings coming out of the courts—they could do nothing. In essence, they would be too smart to make a tax-wise business decision because it may have been contested somewhere, somehow, or at some time before. With no contest—the IRS wins before the process even begins.

Business Profit Requirement—the Truth

Let's go back to Joe's underwater photography business. Joe probably would have received the typical response that many accountants and tax professionals give concerning the deductibility of business expenses, i.e., "NO WAY!" Their number one question would be, "What about the hobby laws?"—"You have to make a profit!" After all, they have an excuse because this is what they have been taught, and besides it is safer for them to just say no.

The truth is that there are no business profit requirements. There are numerous cases on the books involving artists who deducted the cost of their materials as a business expense while they waited for years to make a sale. Even so, they were losing money all that time.

☑ The actual standard is that you need to have a profit *expectation*. Even when the hobby laws are applicable, they do not apply to every situation. If they did, there would never have been the explosion of the new economy with its "dot.com" startups. We will explore the hobby laws in greater detail later in the book, but knowing that it is not as ominous as so many "experts" suggest should provide more opportunities for tax-wise business owners.

Holdbacks

Sometimes the line between personal deductions and business deductions becomes blurred. To avoid a perceived problem, the uninformed and ill-advised taxpayer will miss a tax-wise opportunity. Even some accountants and tax professionals do not realize that you can apportion the deduction to give credence to the fact that the expense was not solely business related. The Code allows taxpayers to allocate a portion of the expense as business and a portion as personal.

Note: Tax-savvy accountants will sometimes "hold back" a percentage of business expenses as a safety margin in case of an audit. If the IRS tries to argue that a claimed business expense may be personal and therefore disallowed, the accountant will inform the IRS agent that he missed several deductions and request a refund for his client. He might start the discussion with the IRS agent by saying, "Thanks for the audit, I forgot to deduct . . . ." After which, the agent would probably think twice about spending too much time on reviewing the client's records. At least in this case, an audit may not be all that bad.

The point is that taxation is not an exact science. Schools that train tax advisors typically keep their students focused between the very bright lines formed by literal interpretations of the Code which usually emphasize personal rather than business taxation. The institutions often do not have the time to present the vast array of business tax rule interpretations, nor do many of the graduates ever have a chance to gain experience in these areas. This lack of training and experience should cause all business owners some concern. While they may want to listen to their accountants and tax professionals, only tax-wise business owners can be sure that the advice they receive is not too conservative or even wrong. It just is not possible to know whether you have a good accountant or tax professional—unless you have at least a basic understanding about the areas in which you seek their advice.

The U.S. Government Accountability Office has reviewed paid preparers repeatedly over the years to determine accuracy rates and the general well-being of the paid preparer industry (hint: not so good as it has no real regulation). The IRS Return Preparer Initiative was implemented by the IRS in an attempt to regulate the paid preparer industry by requiring competency testing, continuing education and oversight, but the rules were ultimately struck down in court as the IRS exceeded its granted authority (see: *Loving v. IRS,* 742 F.3d 1013 (D.C. Cir. 2014)). As a result, most taxpayers do not realize that the individual to whom they are bringing complex tax matters to and seeking advice may have no formal education or tax background. In short, it is really up to the taxpayer to know enough about the tax system and its laws to determine if the preparer with whom they are working is competent.

Know How to Ask the Question

☑ I will close this chapter with a little self-effacing humor about my legal profession and accountants. It illustrates the importance of knowing enough to ask the right questions. As I have said earlier, this is extremely important when dealing with your tax advisors. Without this knowledge and skill, it is impossible to be a tax-wise business owner.

There was a man who decided to go on a hot air balloon ride. He lifted off and everything was fine until the weather became bad and the winds sent him off course. After what seemed like an eternity, the man came across a small farm with a farmer out in the field.

The man lowered his hot air balloon and called out to the farmer, "Excuse me sir, but could you please tell me where I am?"

The farmer, very much surprised by the question, called back, "You are in a hot air balloon over my field."

The man in the hot air balloon was not amused—he called back "You must be an accountant (insert "attorney" if you so desire) because the information you gave me was completely accurate, yet utterly worthless."

Notes

1. U.S. Master Tax Guide, CCH, Inc., 1992: 184.
2. IRC, §469(e)(1).
3. IRC, §469(c)(1).
4. Remember- "deductible" means that the expense is subtracted from your total, or gross, income. What is left is referred to as your "net profit" or "earnings."

CHAPTER

The Business Framework

"If you don't know where you are going, every road will get you nowhere."

—*Henry Kissinger*

The most important tax-wise decision that you will make in connection with your business is the legal form (also referred to as legal or business "entity" or "structure") in which you will operate. Choosing it is a complex issue because of the inherent taxation and liability consequences that directly result from this decision.

The form that is best for a situation depends on:

- ☐ The potential liability involved in the endeavor, and
- ☐ The after-tax, wealth-building results the business owner wants to achieve.

Sometimes owners have a choice; at other times, the circumstances limit them to a single legal form. Even then, as time passes, they may decide to change the structure to conform to their changing business and personal goals.

Owners of established businesses may believe that it is superfluous to learn about other legal structures for conducting their endeavors. However, they are very wrong! The cost and inconvenience of restructuring a business and/or using other legal structures for a particular endeavor may be a small, tax-wise price to pay. In fact it may be the only way for tax-wise business owners to reach their ultimate goal of building substantial personal and family wealth.

> *"Lots of times you have to pretend to join a parade in which you're not really interested in order to get where you're going.*
>
> —George Morley

☑ Tax-wise business owners need to know the attributes and shortcomings of each of the business entity options. Armed with this knowledge, they will be able to discuss their situation intelligently with an attorney or tax expert who will aid them in making the right selection and complying with the applicable legal and taxation requirements.

This chapter provides an overview and comparison of the basic business structures available to owners. Tax-wise owners can use this information to guide them at the outset of any new venture; and they may also want to refer to it periodically as their businesses reach different stages of development.

Defining Parameters

There are two distinctions between business structures that need to be identified and explained so that the important attributes and limitations of the legal forms of doing business can be understood and compared.

Flow-Through Taxation

From the business owner's standpoint, the most important tax distinction between the legal forms is the difference between a "flow-through" and a "stand-alone" entity.

From a taxation perspective, a "flow-through" business entity is not legally separate from the person who owns it. Therefore, at income tax time, the owner reports all business income or losses on his individual income tax return. The business itself is not taxed. The IRS refers to this as "flow-through" or "pass-through" taxation because the profits/losses flow through the business to the owner's tax return. That is, the owners, not the business entity, ultimately pay the taxes or write off the losses.

There are two primary tax advantages to utilizing flow-through taxation as opposed to having the business entity pay its own taxes.

1. In the case of profits, taxes are paid only once—by the business owner—rather than twice (i.e., first by the business entity and then by the owner upon receipt of dividends or other forms of income from the business).
2. If the business loses money, the losses can be used by the owner to offset any taxable income that he has earned from other sources.

The term "flow-through" entity applies to any business that is taxed under either Subchapter K or Subchapter S of the IRC, including: sole proprietorships, general and limited partnerships, "S" corporations, and certain limited liability companies.

Limited Liability

Another basic but nontax related distinction between legal forms of doing business is the difference between those that provide their owners with "limited liability" and those that do not. "Limited liability" basically means that the owner's personal wealth and assets are protected. They may not be attached by the courts in order to pay business debts or financial judgments levied solely against the business.

A decision by an owner to use a legal entity for doing business that provides him with limited liability will most certainly affect how the business is run. Although these entities are somewhat more complex to run, they do not leave an owner personally vulnerable to business lawsuits and debts.

Legal entities that provide business owners with varying degrees of "limited liability" are corporations (both C and S corporations), partnerships [for limited (passive) partners], limited liability partnerships, and limited liability companies.

Legal Structures

Under the governing laws of all states, there are five legal structures that are most commonly used for conducting business.

- ☐ Sole proprietorships
- ☐ Partnerships (general and limited)
- ☐ Corporations (C, S, personal service)
- ☐ Limited liability companies
- ☐ Joint ventures

Each of the business forms has a very specific, complex, and unique set of federal recognition rules and associated taxes. While most of the major benefits and drawbacks of each structure will be covered, the lists are in no way exhaustive. Under any given set of circumstances, the benefits and/or the disadvantages of a particular legal form of doing business may become more or less pronounced. Thus it is important to understand the concepts being discussed and to seek the advice of competent legal and taxation professionals.

Sole Proprietorship

Definition

For tax purposes, the term "sole proprietorship" is an individual (or a husband and wife who elect not to be taxed as a partnership) who owns an unincorporated enterprise that is operated with a profit motive. In other words, if you begin a business and do not create a formal entity, e.g., corporation or limited liability company, you are a "sole proprietor."

Black's Law Dictionary defines a sole proprietorship as:

A form of business in which one person owns all of the assets of the business in contrast to a partnership, trust or corporation. *The sole proprietor is solely liable for all of the debts of the business.*

Operations

Sole proprietorship status is limited to businesses that are owned by a single person or a married couple (either in a community property state or who choose to be treated as a "qualified joint venture") under certain circumstances.

The main advantage of sole proprietorships is their simplicity. They are easy to set up and run—so easy that many people own sole proprietorships and do not even know it. For instance, freelance photographers and writers, craftsmen who take jobs on a contract basis, and salesmen who receive only commissions are all automatically sole proprietors. (This is true whether or not an owner has a regular day job.)

Liability

Because there is really no line between the sole proprietor and his business:

- ☐ The owner has no protection from the liabilities incurred in business activities;
- ☐ The business assets are at risk in a personal lawsuit filed against the owner.

However, some states may allow protection of personal assets that are owned jointly with a spouse or are transferred outright to a spouse or children. (Seek legal advice if you are counting on these tactics to limit your business liabilities.) In addition, insurance is often available to cover some of the risks of a sole proprietorship, although it may be expensive and the coverage may be very limited.

If liability concerns are an issue, business owners should consider other legal structures for their endeavors.

Taxation

As far as the IRS is concerned, no federal forms, filings, or licenses of any kind are required to start a sole proprietorship. From their perspective, the business starts the first day that it receives income from providing goods and services.

The IRC considers an owner and his business as one and the same entity—therefore, the business does not file its own tax return. The tax liabilities for the business are filed on the sole proprietor's individual return. This may simplify reporting, but is severely limits the amount of tax planning that can be done. For example, there is only one fiscal year-end, and there is no way to retain profits in the company.

Expenses

Under the IRC, all legitimate business expenses can be deducted no matter what legal form a business takes. The types of expenses and rules for deducting expenses are covered in Chapter 5.

Profits

Sole proprietors are taxed on all profits in the year they are earned—whether they take the money out of the business or not. This means that all profits are taxed as if the business owner had put them in his own pocket, even if the money is in the business's checking and savings accounts.

Losses

One of the benefits of being a sole proprietor is that losses can offset the owner's other sources of income. The business losses may be used to offset the sole proprietor's interest income, capital gains, or even spousal income. However, claiming this business loss offset is subject to the "hobby loss" rules under IRC 183.

> . . . *activities not engaged in for profit by individuals or S corporations are not allowed in business deductions* . . .

The presumption is that businesses are engaged in activities "for profit"—if their gross income exceeds expense deductions for three out of five consecutive taxable years. In other words, sole proprietors need to make money three out of five years if they want to be eligible to use business losses to offset their personal income. (Note: C corporations are not subject to this rule.)

Tax-Reporting

The net profit of the business is reported on a separate "schedule" (form), Schedule C (Schedule F for farming), and attached to the owner's individual, annual filing of Form 1040 or 1040-EZ. A separate Schedule C must be filed for each business that you or your spouse own and operate. A husband and wife who run a sole proprietorship together must file two separate Schedule C forms with their Form 1040 (otherwise they are considered a partnership and must file a partnership return, Form 1065).

The IRS states that an unincorporated business jointly owned by a married couple is generally classified as a partnership for federal tax purposes. A "qualified joint venture," whose only members are a husband and a wife filing a joint return, can elect not to be treated as a partnership for federal tax purposes [*See Co-ownership below*].

Finally, filing a schedule C significantly increases the sole proprietor's chance of an audit.[1] The IRS has reached various conclusions about sole proprietors. These include a belief that sole proprietors are likely to understate their income while overstating their expenses. Obviously sole proprietors have a greater opportunity to omit income and claim personal expenses as "business deductions." This makes them an attractive target for tax audits.

Self-Employment Taxes

The IRS classifies sole proprietors as self-employed individuals who must pay quarterly estimated income taxes, as well as self-employment tax for social security and Medicare contributions. The self-employment tax is twice the wage earner's social security plus the Medicare withholding rate of 7.65%. These two taxes are paid by the employee and matched by the employer on a dollar-for-dollar basis—each paying 6.2% for social security (on $118,500 or less in 2015) and 1.45% for Medicare based on the employee's gross wages. A sole proprietor on the other hand must pay both the employee's and employer's portions of social security and Medicare taxes. This is why these combined taxes are referred to as the self-employment tax (SE tax).

This self-employment tax is assessed at 12.4% (the social security portion) of the first $118,500 (2015 upper limit) of self-employment earnings, plus 2.9% of all self-employment earnings for Medicare. Therefore, in 2015, the SE tax is 15.3%

for amounts of $118,500 or less, plus 2.9% of the amount of self-employment earnings over $118,500. If your net earnings exceed $118,500, you will continue to pay only the Medicare portion of the Social Security tax, which is 2.9%. Beginning in 2013, the Medicare tax rate for net earnings in excess of $200,000 ($250,000 for joint filers) is 3.8%.

Normally, both employees and employers must pay the OASDI (Old Age, Survivors, and Disability Income) portion of federal payroll tax at a 6.2% on wages up to the annual "wage base."

The Tax Relief, Unemployment Insurance Reauthorization, and Job Creation Act of 2010 created a payroll tax holiday in 2011. After legislation extending the tax break through 2012, the payroll tax holiday expired in January 2013. As a result, the social security contribution rate for employees went back to the standard of 6.2%. The contribution rate for self-employed workers increased from 10.4% to 12.4%. These increases set the contribution rates back to the levels that had been in effect prior to 2011. The 2016 limits are $118,500.

SE tax is computed on Schedule SE. If a sole proprietor is also employed by someone else, he must use the long form of Schedule SE to ensure that he does not pay more social security tax than required since this tax has already been withheld from his salary by his employer. Although SE taxes are not allowable business expenses, some tax relief is allowed. One-half of the sole proprietor's SE taxes are deductible as adjustments to gross income on the owner's Form 1040 or 1040-EZ. This write-off reduces his adjusted gross income and ultimately results in a reduction in income taxes.

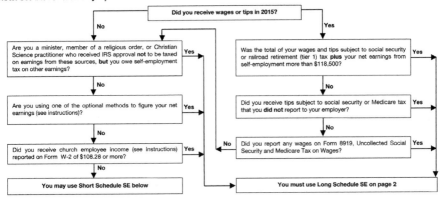

IRS Form 1040 Schedule SE

The self-employment tax is no small matter, and it is an additional tax that is above and beyond the other income taxes that the sole proprietor must pay.

Co-Ownership

The IRS says that unless a business meets the requirements listed below to be a qualified joint venture, a sole proprietorship must be *solely owned by one spouse*. The other spouse can work in the business as an employee. A business jointly owned and operated by a husband and wife is a partnership, unless the spouses qualify and elect to have the business be treated as a Qualified Joint Venture, or they operate their business in one of the nine community property states [Arizona, California, Idaho, Louisiana, Nevada, New Mexico, Texas, Washington, and Wisconsin.]

A married couple who jointly own and operate a trade or business may choose for each spouse to be treated as a sole proprietor by electing to file as a "qualified joint venture." Requirements for a qualified joint venture:

- ☐ The only members in the joint venture are a husband and wife who file a joint tax return,
- ☐ The trade or business is owned and operated by the spouses as co-owners (and not in the name of a state law entity such as an LLC or LLP),
- ☐ The husband and wife must each materially participate in the trade or business, and
- ☐ Both spouses must elect qualified joint venture status on Form 1040 by dividing the items of income, gain, loss, deduction, credit and expenses in accordance with their respective interests in such venture and each spouse filing with the Form 1040 a separate Schedule C), Schedule C-EZ, or Form 4835, and, if required, a separate Schedule SE to pay self-employment tax.

Changing the Business

While the vast majority (80%) of businesses start and end as sole proprietorships, others are transformed along the way. Usually a business owner goes to the expense and effort of changing the business structure in order to address liability issues, meet estate-planning goals, take on partners, bring in public and private financing, etc. Seldom is a change from sole proprietorship to another legal structure caused by a single factor.

Ending the Business

Voluntarily ending a sole proprietorship is as easy as starting one—simply stop doing business and file the last Schedule C (with the words "Final Return" written across the top) along with the 1040 return. However, disposing of the business assets is not as easy. When the assets or the business itself are sold, the owner must report on his tax return the gain (or loss) for each individual item that is included in the sale.

Death and Taxes

A sole proprietorship dies with its owner. This places the business directly into the sole proprietor's estate, where its value may be subject to estate taxes and probate. Here, as with any transformation or sale of a sole proprietorship, competent legal and tax advice is often essential.

Sole Proprietorship Example

Ed Smith decides to go into business for himself. He buys the necessary tools and sets up shop as "Ed Smith's Mobile Motorcycle Repair." Ed travels around the state and fixes motorcycles for $50 per hour, and he deducts all of his tools and expenses. Here is a statement of his income and deductible expenses in his first year along with the calculation for his self-employment taxes:

Gross earnings	$63,000
Deductible expenses	
Tools	($4,000)
Accountant	($1,000)
Travel (10,000 miles @32.5 cents)	($325)
Meals (50% of $500.00)	($250)
Manuals	($100)
Business phone	($1,200)
Advertising	($300)
Net taxable income	$55,825 $55,825
Self-employment tax	
($55,825 x 15.3% = $8,541)	
Deduction for one-half of self-employment tax	
($55,825 x 50%)[2]	($4,271)
Standard deduction with 3 exemptions	($23,900)
(3 x $3,900 for 2013)	
Taxable income	$27,654
Income tax (2013 tax tables, married)	($)
Net after-tax take home	$36,829
Nondeductible expenses	
Medical expenses	
(over 7% AGI is deductible)	($2,000)
Remaining monies	$34,829

What is clear is that Ed's biggest cost of doing business is his taxes. Luckily, he was able to deduct several of his business expenses ($7,175).

Note: As a sole proprietor, Ed was not able to claim his medical expenses as a business deduction. However, if he employed his spouse, he could have his business provide a medical plan as a nontaxable fringe benefit. Ed would then be able to receive a portion of the benefit through the medical coverage extended to his spouse. Unfortunately, in 2015, Ed would also have to pay a 6.0% federal unemployment tax on the first $7,000 in wages paid to his spouse.

These tax consequences apply while Ed is alive. When Ed passes away, the entire value of his business would be included in his estate and subject to estate taxes. Unfortunately, if Ed built a business of significant worth, most of the value would end up in the hands of Uncle Sam.[3]

Advantages of Sole Proprietorships

- ☐ The owner has exclusive control over the business.
- ☐ Compared with other business entities, this is the simplest and least expensive to form.
- ☐ Profits pass directly to the owner without taxation at the business level.

Disadvantages of Sole Proprietorships

- ☐ The owner has unlimited personal liability for business lawsuits and mistakes made by employees and/or agents.
- ☐ A sole proprietorship must be dissolved upon the death or bankruptcy of the owner.

Partnerships

Partnerships are legal business structures that are jointly owned by two or more parties who have agreed to share the profits, losses, assets, and liabilities in some proportionate manner. However, partnerships are not taxable entities under federal law, i.e., there are no income taxes assessed at the partnership level. For tax purposes, business income and expenses pass through the partnership to the partners.

Partnerships are one of the most flexible forms of business because a partner's interest in profits can be different from his proportionate share of any loss. In addition, when a partner contributes an asset to a partnership, he gives up ownership of that specific property in exchange for an equity interest in all partnership assets. These and other features of partnerships often make partnerships ideal estate- and wealth-building structures for the tax-wise business owner.

Definition

At its most basic level, a partnership is a business that is owned by two or more persons. The term "person" can include individuals, corporations, other partnerships, trusts, and any of the many other legally recognized business entities. Typically, two or more parties combine capital and/or services into the partnership for the purpose of carrying on profit-making activities.

Internal Revenue Code section 761 defines partnerships as:

> . . . a syndicate, pool, joint venture or other unincorporated organization through or by means of which any business, financial operation, or venture is carried on, and which is not . . . a corporation or a trust or estate.

Legal Status

State law regulates the formation and operation of partnerships. Fortunately, all states, except Louisiana, have adopted the Uniform Partnership Act (UPA) or Revised Uniform Partnership Act (RUPA). so partnership laws are very similar throughout the United States.

The law usually treats activities of a partnership as if these activities were actually performed by each partner acting independently. Essentially, the partnership and each partner are treated as a single legal entity—except to the extent that the partnership itself can hold and convey real property, and it can sue or be sued in its own name. In addition, in bankruptcy procedures, the partnership is unaffected by the bankruptcy of a partner, and vice versa.

Agreements

Partnerships may be oral or in writing. A good partnership agreement is complex since it needs to contemplate all possible business situations the partners may encounter. In addition, it must cover the resolution of possible conflicts, allow for the orderly succession in interest, and dissolution.

Some of the many items that should be covered in a written partnership agreement include:

- ☐ Capital contributions by the partners;
- ☐ Management and voting rights of partners;
- ☐ Profit and loss sharing arrangements;
- ☐ Conflict resolution procedures;
- ☐ Admission of new partners;

- ☐ Authority to bind the partnership contractually and financially;
- ☐ Buy-sell agreements; and
- ☐ Disposition of interest on the death of a partner or dissolution.

In the absence of a partnership agreement or if a specific provision is missing from an agreement, the UPA or RUPA laws of the state where the partnership was created will become the standard. They are the guides that define the rights and responsibilities of partners in that state. Should the partners desire, they can choose not to follow these standards—but this requires a formal, written, partnership agreement.

Partnership law is very complex. Therefore, ask an attorney to prepare your partnership agreement, or at the very least, carefully review the document that you draft yourself. Although the partnership agreement must be appropriate for the size and formality of the business, this is not an area to skimp on resources. A little more time, effort, and money spent on the partnership agreement may be the key to a smooth, harmonious, and successful business. By seeking advice from your legal and tax professionals early on, you may be able to prevent big partnership headaches later.

Taxation of Partnerships

For tax purposes, all of the income or loss of any partnership must be reported as distributions to the partners annually. All partnerships must file a Form 1065 with the IRS each year. Although this is only an informational return, it is due within three months and 15 days of the end of the partnership's fiscal year.[4] All partnerships also must provide each of their partners with a Schedule K-1 that delineates that partner's distributive share of the partnership's income or loss. Each partner reports his share of partnership income or loss on his Form 1040 using the information from the Schedule K-1 that was provided to him or her by the partnership.

From a taxation perspective, all partnership profits and losses flow through to the partners with no tax at the partnership level. The character of the income or loss remains the same as it passes through the partnership to each partner.[5] For example, if the partnership's income is from long-term capital gains, it flows down to each partner as long-term capital gains income.

The manner that income or losses are filed on a partner's tax return largely depends on that partner's legal structure, basis in the partnership, at-risk rules, and passive activity rules. These topics will be explored in greater detail later in this book.

☑ A note of caution: Partners are liable for taxes on partnership profits, regardless of whether the monies distributed to the partners by the partnership are sufficient to pay the tax.

General Partnership

A general partnership is the simplest partnership to start because it can be formed by conduct alone, i.e., the agreement between partners does not have to be in writing. In fact, a general partnership exists whenever two or more parties join together to carry on a trade or business. There are no other requirements.

Operations

In a general partnership (absent of agreement to the contrary):

- ☐ Every partner has an equal right in the management and control of the business;
- ☐ Any partner can obligate the partnership to a contract, debt, or other transaction that is within the scope of the business;
- ☐ The partnership is dissolved upon the death or bankruptcy of a partner.

Liabilities

General partners are "jointly and severally" liable. This means that each partner is responsible for *all* debts, obligations, and liabilities of the partnership, regardless of his proportionate interest in the business. In any legal or creditor action against a general partnership, a claimant can satisfy his claim from all or any one of the partners. Each partner can be sued personally, and his respective assets and bank accounts attached. If one general partner has more wealth and personal assets that the other partners, he risks losing everything—even if the other partners were the cause of the lawsuit. Similarly, general partners are also "jointly and severally" liable for the mistakes or negligence of the partnership's employees and agents.

Taxation

General partners are not employees of the partnership and cannot receive salaries from the partnership. They are considered self-employed and working for their own business. Payments from the partnership to general partners can be in the form of loans, fringe benefits, advances against profits, or guaranteed amounts. None of these funds are ever reported on a W-2 form, as in the case of employees—nor are they reported on a Form 1099, as would payments to independent contractors. All amounts given to general partners are reported annually on their respective Schedule K-1s. These sums are subject to self-employment tax as explained under "Sole Proprietorship" earlier in this chapter.

Losses are also passed through to general partners and reported on their respective Schedule K-1s. They are claimed on each partner's individual return. However, claims for losses cannot exceed the general partner's "basis" in the partnership. "Basis" is the sum total of the fair market value of assets plus all monies that a general partner has contributed to the partnership.

General Partnership Example

Ed, John, and Sally form a general partnership and begin a software development venture (EJS Partnership). They each contribute funds to start the business and receive the following interest:

	Capital Contribution	Partnership Interest
Ed	$50,000	50%
John	$25,000	25%
Sally	$25,000	25%

EJS Partnership is very profitable in its first year, netting $200,000. Each partner received a K-1 Form that showed his or her respective share of the income.

	Partnership Interest	K-1 Form Income
Ed	50%	$100,000
John	25%	$50,000
Sally	25%	$50,000

☑ Remember: Partnership profits do not have to be distributed, but they must always be reported as income on each partner's tax return.

Advantages of General Partnerships

- ☐ The formation costs are relatively inexpensive.
- ☐ There are few legal requirements prior to startup.
- ☐ All partners have an equal right to manage and control.
- ☐ There are no taxes at the general partnership level—single taxation on profits.
- ☐ Partners have a high degree of flexibility in drafting the covenants of their general partnership agreement.

Disadvantages of General Partnerships

- ☐ Partners have unlimited personal liability.
- ☐ Any partner has the authority to bind the partnership.

- ☐ Every partner has an equal right to manage and control.
- ☐ Tax liabilities pass to partners even if there are no partnership distributions.
- ☐ In the absence of a formal agreement, partners may not be able to transfer their interests without the consent of all existing partners.
- ☐ Limited duration—the partnership is dissolved on death or bankruptcy of a partner, absent other provisions in the partnership agreement.

Limited Partnership

In most respects general and limited partnerships are quite similar. The most important difference is that limited partnerships have two classes of partners—general partners and limited partners.

General Partners

The general partners manage the day-to-day activities of the partnership. As in a general partnership, they are jointly and severally liable for all debts incurred by the partnership and all claims arising from lawsuits.

Limited Partners

The limited partners are not personally responsible for the obligations of the partnership to third-party creditors. Therefore, the liability of these partners is limited to the capital contributions they make to the partnership. In exchange for this limited liability status, a limited partner may not, by law, exercise any significant level of control over the affairs of the partnership.

Formation

In most jurisdictions, limited partnership agreements are required to be in writing. This document contains the same provisions as a general partnership agreement—with several complex additions that are specific to limited partners. Generally, a Certificate of Limited Partnership must be signed and filed with the Secretary of State or another appropriate state office. Until these state-mandated requirements are met, the partnership is treated as a general partnership—thereby exposing all limited partners to unlimited personal liability. Because of the required filings and organizational complexities, forming a limited partnership usually requires professional legal guidance and may be relatively expensive.

Taxation

A limited partnership reports income and losses and is taxed the same way as a general partnership. All income and losses pass through to partners and are reported on the same Form 1065 and Schedule K-1 documents.

The general partners of a limited partnership report partnership income and losses exactly like they would for a general partnership. (Refer to the taxation section under "General Partnership" in this chapter.)

By law, limited partners do not manage, control, or work for the limited partnership. As such, their distributed share of partnership income is not subject to self-employment tax.

However, limited partners are subject to a special set of rules for claiming the losses that are reported on their respective Schedule K-1s. These highly complex rules are explained in IRS Publication 925, "Passive Activity and At-Risk Rules." These "PAL rules" effectively restrict limited partners from deducting limited partnership losses that exceed their total "passive activity" income from all sources.

Expanded Uses

Historically, limited partnerships have been created because a general partner wants to secure additional financing, or he wants to spread the risk of a venture by taking in more partners. However, these new partners may want to invest and share in the profits or take tax deductions for losses, but without the risk of unlimited personal liability. Limited partnerships have grown in popularity because they are very flexible and effective tools for holding appreciating assets—from the standpoint of tax reduction and asset protection.

Tax Reduction

An important aspect of partnerships is the division that they create between personal assets and those that are owned by the partnership. For example, if real property is transferred to a partnership in exchange for an interest in the partnership, the partner no longer owns the real property, the partnership does. This is an important concept for tax purposes because the taxes associated with the transferred property now flows through the partnership and are distributed proportionately to each of the partners.

If this exchange of real property for partnership interest occurs in a limited partnership, the transferring partner may have a variety of tax strategies available that can lawfully reduce his or her current tax situation. In addition, the transfer of the real property to a limited partnership effectively lowers the value of the transferees' estate—thus reducing or eliminating a major portion of the estate taxes that might otherwise be due upon the death of that partner. This process, as well as other tax-wise, asset-transfer tactics for business owners are discussed in Chapter 5.

There is another tax benefit that is unique to limited partnerships. It results from the form that limited partnership income is passed through to limited partners. Because limited partners do not participate in the management and control of the business, their partnership earnings are classified as "passive" income.

The business income that is passed down to limited partners is not subject to self-employment taxes. This results in a potential tax savings of up to 15.3% of the income distribution. (Refer to the "Sole Proprietorship" section in this chapter.) Real property owners or other tax-wise business owners can transform the tax classification of the income they receive by using this aspect of limited partnerships.

Asset Protection

Limited partnerships are also a powerful and effective asset protection tool. As discussed earlier, when a limited partner transfers assets into a partnership, these assets become the property of the limited partnership. Thus, if that limited partner is ever sued personally, the transferred assets are outside the reach of the creditor. Courts recognize these assets as limited partnership property. As such, the outside creditors of the individual partners are limited to "charging orders," or what is essentially a subrogated interest in the transferred property. At best, the creditors will be entitled to "stand in the shoes" of the limited partner for partnership purposes. This means that, should the limited partnership distribute profits, the creditor would receive compensation as if he or she was the limited partner. However, if the limited partnership decides not to distribute profits (this decision is usually at the discretion of the general partner), the creditor could remain liable for the taxes on that limited partner's proportionate share of the undistributed limited partnership income. (Ouch!)

Advantages of Limited Partnerships

- ☐ Limited partners are protected from personal liability.
- ☐ General partners retain all management and control.
- ☐ There is a high degree of flexibility in the distribution of income and losses.
- ☐ Limited partner's interests are freely transferable.
- ☐ There are no taxes at the limited partnership level.
- ☐ The death or bankruptcy of a limited partner has no effect on the partnership status (unless you have a poorly drafted partnership agreement).

Disadvantages of Limited Partnerships

- ☐ Formation is legally complex and relatively expensive.
- ☐ Limited partners are subject to "passive activity and at-risk rules."

- [ ] General partners have unlimited personal liability.
- [ ] Tax liabilities pass to partners even if there are no partnership distributions.

Corporations

Definition

A corporation is a legal entity that is separate and apart from its owners (shareholders). For many, the term "corporation" brings up images of multi-national empires with massive business assets and thousands of employees. The fact is that most corporations are not extremely large and can be as small as one person. The simplest way to envision a corporation is to think of it as specific legal structure that exists only for business purposes. The law refers to a corporation as a "juristic person"—meaning a person in the eye of the law, but not a living or natural person. As such, a corporation has the capacity to sue and be sued—as well as to own, buy, sell, lease, and mortgage property in its own name. It owns the assets of a business, is liable for the debts and legal obligations of that business, and is perpetual—meaning that it does not have a life span and can therefore outlive its owners.

Black's Law Dictionary defines a corporation as follows:

> *An artificial person or legal entity created by or under the authority of the laws of a state. An association of persons created by statute as a legal entity. The law treats the corporation itself as a person that can sue and be sued. The corporation is distinct from the individuals who comprise it (shareholders). The corporation survives the death of its investors . . .*

"That must be wonderful; I don't understand it at all."
—MOLIÈRE, 1622

Formation

Forming a corporation is more complicated and more expensive than forming a sole proprietorship or a general partnership. Almost all corporations are created under state statutes. The specific aspects of forming a corporation vary from state to state; however, every state requires that Articles of Incorporation be filed for approval with its Secretary of State's office or another appropriate state office. Once approved, the state issues a Certificate of Incorporation to the organizers.

Corporations do not need to be formed (incorporated) in the state in which the business operates. For example, many corporations are formed in the states of Delaware and Nevada because these states have corporate laws that encourage businesses to incorporate there. Regardless of where a corporation is incorporated, it is usually required to formally register in the states where it is doing business. In the same light, the corporation may be subject to taxes on income generated in those states.

Operation

Corporations are further distinguished from sole proprietorships or partnerships because they issue capital stock (which represents incremental ownership of the company) to their owners (shareholders or stockholders).

> Shareholders own the corporation. They have no personal liability for the acts of the corporation or

its directors, officers, managers, or employees. The only liability shareholders have is for the amount of money they paid for stock. Shareholders do not have any direct control over the daily operations of the business, but they do elect the directors of the corporation.

The board of directors is responsible for managing the affairs of the corporation. The directors make the major corporate decisions and appoint the officers of the corporation. They are generally protected from liability for their business decisions.

Officers manage the daily affairs of the corporation. The number of officers required varies from state to state, but a president, vice president, treasurer, and secretary are typical. Most states allow for several offices to be held by the same person.

Most states require that a corporation conduct annual meetings of directors and shareholders. To maintain corporate status, directors must conduct these meetings, properly document the proceedings, and meet all other statutory requirements. Failure to comply with these complex regulations will result in the removal of shareholders, officers, and directors from the veil of liability protection offered to them through incorporation.

Expense Deductions

Corporations receive preferential tax treatment when it comes to expense deductions that are standard and recognized by the IRS. This is particularly relevant to business owners who are thinking about incorporating. Here are a few standard corporate expense deductions that are allowed by the IRS as offsets against income:

Accounting & bookkeeping	Advertising
Airplanes, boat(s)	Assistants
Automobiles	Bad debts
Bonuses	Books
Burglar alarm systems	Business consultants
Business licenses	Business seminars
Certified audits	Charitable contributions
Commission paid to salesmen	Contract labor
Convention & hotel expenses	Copyright(s)
Depletion	Depreciation
Directors fees	Disability plans
Dividend exclusion	Dues to professional organizations
Electricity	Entertainment (50% deductible)
Filing expenses	Financial consultants
Finders' fees	Fire arms, ammunition (for corp. security)
Fire/flood/hurricane losses	General business insurance
Incorporating costs	Insurance
Interest	Internet
Invoicing	Legal fees
Life insurance	Limited partnership costs
Local transportation	Logo(s)
Losses in business	Maintenance
Medical reimbursement plan	Newspapers, magazines
Office equipment	State industrial insurance

Liability

Piercing the corporate veil. Because the law views a corporation as a separate and distinct legal entity, corporate shareholders are generally not responsible for debts and obligations of the corporation. However, if the veil of corporate protection is pierced, directors, officers, and shareholders may find that they are personally responsible for the past, present, and future creditors and tax liabilities of the business.

Corporations are excellent liability insulators for owners of businesses. If a corporation is sued, it is the corporation—not its owners—that is subject to judgment claims and/or the claims of creditors. This limitation of personal liability is one of the most significant advantages of the corporate structure. There can, however, be exceptions to the "limited liability" concept. Specifically, when certain minimum requirements of maintaining a corporation have not been met (such as keeping proper records, holding required meetings, and so forth), or when the owners have committed criminal or fraudulent acts, courts may "pierce the corporate veil." This means that courts may disregard the corporate structure and impose personal liability on the owners as though no corporation existed. Provided that owners do not incorporate in order to commit criminal or fraudulent acts, and if they comply with the state's minimal corporate maintenance requirements—then owners need not be overly concerned about this occurring.

Just as owners have the right to limit their personal liabilities for business activities, corporations also keep business assets separate from the owner's personal affairs. This means that the corporation's assets are shielded from liabilities for the owner's personal acts. Think of how restrictive the business world would be if there were no ways to limit liability. Medical research, alternative energy development, or even the act of hiring employees would all be thwarted by the threat of judgments that might be levied against the owners of the business. If this were so, and the owners were potentially liable, people who owned one business would be afraid to venture into another for fear that a lawsuit against one would topple the other. Fortunately, even though each state has tailored its liability exposure rules somewhat differently, corporations in all states typically reduce personal liability exposure and therefore provide a useful mechanism for allowing businesses to get started and to grow.

There are two broad classifications of corporations: "S" corporations and "C" corporations. The primary distinction between the two is in their respective tax treatment for federal income tax purposes.

C Corporation

A C corporation is also known as a regular corporation. The "C" means that the corporation is taxed under Subchapter C of the IRC. There are no limitations on the number of shareholders, and shareholders may be individuals, other corporations, partnerships, limited liability companies, trusts, or nonresident aliens. C corporations may issue several different "classes" of stock (preferred, nonvoting, etc.). Each class of stock may be structured to give different forms of ownership to the respective shareholders. This allows a C corporation to creatively finance its activities, protect itself from unwelcomed takeovers, reward specific classes of shareholders, and utilize other complex corporate business development strategies.

Taxation

A C corporation claims its own deductions as offsets to its income and calculates its tax liabilities on Form 1120, *U.S. Corporation Income Tax Return*. Shareholders of C corporations do not report any of the corporate income or losses and may not claim any of the corporate expense deductions on their individual tax returns. Instead, shareholders of C corporations must report the dividends and other distributions from a C corporation as personal income. For example, if a shareholder is also an employee of a C corporation, the salary he receives is deductible at the corporate level on Form 1120, but the shareholder/employee reports the salary as income on his personal tax return. The same process is true for dividends, except that dividends are not deductible on the corporation's Form 1120. Thus, dividends are taxed as part of income at the corporate level and as personal income to the shareholders.

A key advantage of a C corporation is that it may retain some of its profits for future investment, without the shareholders having to pay tax on the retained earnings. Taxation issues and limitations on retained earnings should be discussed with competent legal and tax advisors.

Double Taxation

Subchapter C mandates that a C corporation is taxed as an entity separate from any of the individuals who owns it. Therefore, all profits of the business are taxed at the corporate level. If some of those profits are passed on to shareholders in the form of distributions or dividends, each shareholder is also obligated to pay ordinary income tax on these amounts. As a result, taxes on the profits of C corporations are paid twice—i.e., "double taxation." Double taxation may be partially or completely avoided in a small business by paying a salary to employee-shareholders. The laws governing this area are complicated and tax-wise business owners should discuss them with their accountants and legal advisors.

The double taxation issue may also apply upon the dissolution of a C corporation. If assets are liquidated and the corporation owes a capital gains tax, the individual shareholders will also recognize a taxable gain passed through in the liquidated distribution.

Many accountants, attorneys, and financial advisors shy away from C corporations for fear of this double taxation. Because a C corporation pays its own taxes, the profits flow out to the shareholders (owners) in the form of after-tax corporate "dividends." The problem with dividends is that the money paid out to the shareholders is not a deductible expense to the corporation. A C corporation pays tax on its income and then distributes dividends to the shareholders, who also pay tax on the money they receive. Dividends are very common for publicly traded corporations since they often boost the stock prices. However, small, closely held corporations rarely (if ever) pay dividends. As you will see in subsequent chapters, these companies have other methods for transferring profits to owners and executives that avoid this onerous double taxation problem.

State Tax

In order to reduce taxes, tax-wise business owners of C corporations who engage in interstate commerce[6] may find it beneficial to locate their headquarters and incorporate in a state that does not have a tax on income. This does not mean that the C corporation does not pay federal taxes, it means that it does not pay state taxes (which can be significant, depending on where you reside). Consult with a competent professional if you think that you would like to utilize a tax-free jurisdiction.

Special Characteristics

C corporations are often ideal for small businesses because, for tax purposes, there is no other business entity that gives owners and executives as many benefits. For example, it is only via a C corporation that 100% of an owner's medical expenses can be nontaxable to the employee and deductible to the corporation. This 100% deductibility is also true for the cost of disability plans and the first $50,000 of premiums paid for each employee under group-term life insurance plans. These fringe benefits are generally not available to "S" corporations, partnerships, or sole proprietorships.

All corporations must file their tax returns by the 15th day of the third month following their tax year. However, only a C corporation has the option to select an end of tax year that is not based on a calendar year. For example, individual taxpayers must use December 31st as the end of their tax year. C corporations, on the other hand, may select an off year-end such as March 31st or some other date. This can be important for shifting income out of a closely held C corporation to a tax-wise business owner at the company's year-end. (This will be discussed in a later chapter.)

Corporate Income Tax Rates

Table 7
Tax Rate Schedule

If taxable income (line 30, Form 1120) on page 1 is:

Over—	But not over—	Tax is:	Of the amount over—
$0	$50,000	15%	$0
50,000	75,000	$ 7,500 + 25%	50,000
75,000	100,000	13,750 + 34%	75,000
100,000	335,000	22,250 + 39%	100,000
335,000	10,000,000	113,900 + 34%	335,000
10,000,000	15,000,000	3,400,000 + 35%	10,000,000
15,000,000	18,333,333	5,150,000 + 38%	15,000,000
18,333,333	.....	35%	0

Advantages of C Corporations

- ☐ Shareholders have limited personal liability.
- ☐ Shareholders' interests are freely transferable.
- ☐ C corporations are generally viewed as more stable than other business entities.
- ☐ Third-party sources (banks and venture capitalists) are more willing to finance C corporations than sole proprietorships or partnerships.
- ☐ The death or bankruptcy of a shareholder has no effect on the corporate status.

Disadvantages of C Corporations

- ☐ Formation is legally complex and the associated cost can be significant.
- ☐ State regulatory requirements must be followed to maintain corporate liability protection.
- ☐ Double taxation—tax liabilities are assessed at the corporate level on income, and then at the shareholder's level on dividends and distributions.

S Corporation

An S corporation is a creation of federal tax laws. The "S" comes from the fact that an S corporation is taxed under Subchapter S of the IRC. For all other purposes, an S corporation is treated in similar fashion as a regular (C) corporation.

An S corporation is incorporated under the same state laws as a C corporation. However, an S corporation is a "closely held" corporation that has made a Subchapter S "election" with the IRS through the filing of Form 2553. This allows the S corporation to be taxed under a special provision of federal tax law that preserves the corporation's limited liability under state law, but avoids federal taxation at the corporate level. Very few states do not recognize a Subchapter S election for state tax purposes. In those states, an S corporation will be taxed at the same state level as a C (regular) corporation. Other states may not impose taxes on corporations.

For most purposes, an S corporation is similar to a C corporation. Both types of corporations must have directors, officers, and shareholders. The difference between these two types of corporations is that an S corporation has elected not to be taxed as a corporation.

Qualifications

To qualify for Subchapter S election, a corporation:

- ☐ Must be incorporated in the United States;
- ☐ Must have all shareholders agree to the election;
- ☐ Cannot be a part of an affiliate group of companies that can file a consolidated tax return;
- ☐ Cannot have more than 100 shareholders, and shareholders are limited to individuals, estates, and certain types of trusts (i.e., shareholders cannot be other C corporations, partnerships, limited liability companies, or nonresident aliens—it can be another S corporation so long as it is made into a QSUB);
- ☐ Must operate on a calendar year-end basis;
- ☐ Can issue only one class of stock—however, voting and nonvoting shares are considered as one class.

Taxation

The annual income and losses of an S corporation are passed through to its shareholders in much the same manner as a partnership passes these items through to its partners. However, there are several key differences between the rules for S corporations and those for partnerships.

One difference is in the way that an S corporation must allocate profits, losses, and other items that are passed through to its shareholders. These items must be allocated according to each shareholder's proportionate ownership in the issued and outstanding shares of stock in the corporation. For example, if a shareholder owns 3,000 shares of stock, representing 38.5% of the total number of issued and outstanding shares, that shareholder must be allocated 38.5% of the losses, profits, etc. This is in direct contrast with the rules for partnerships, wherein, by agreement, partners may be allocated interests in these items that are different from their respective percentage interests in the partnership.

Another difference is that shareholders may also be employees of an S corporation, whereas general partners can never receive salaries from a partnership. This allows an S corporation to employ key shareholders and pay for benefits such as health and disability insurance for its employees. The salary, wages, and benefit costs are generally deductible from corporate income. However, employees of S corporations who own 2% or more of the stock cannot claim their personal benefit costs as a business expense deduction unless it is reported on their W-2 as taxable income. The ability to employ shareholders gives S corporations a way to prioritize payments in favor of key personnel because cash flow and expenses can be controlled prior to passing annual profits and losses pro rata to all S corporation shareholders.

Just like partnerships, from a taxation perspective, all S corporation profits and losses flow down to the shareholders with no tax at the corporate level. The character of the income or loss remains the same as it passes through the S corporation to each shareholder.[7] For example, if the S corporation's income is from long-term capital gains, it flows down to each shareholder as long-term capital gains income.

Payments to shareholders are never reported on a W-2 form, except in the case of shareholders/employees—nor are they reported on a Form 1099, as would payments to independent contractors. All amounts given to shareholders are reported annually on their respective Schedule K-1s. The manner that income or losses are filed on a shareholder's tax return largely depends on the character of the income or loss, at-risk rules, and passive activity rules.

If a company does not produce substantial profit, it may be wise to organize it under Subchapter S. The profits would then be added to each owner's personal income and taxed at his/her respective individual tax rates. This may be a tax-saving move when compared with double taxation under a C corporation.

Advantages of S Corporations

- ☐ S corporations have the same limited liability, centralized management, and continuity of existence advantages as C corporations.
- ☐ No double taxation—tax liabilities are not assessed at the corporate level.
- ☐ Favorable capital gains treatment—capital gains are passed through to shareholders without changing the character of the gain. Therefore, shareholders pay taxes at capital gains rates (15%, or 0% for those otherwise in the 10% or 15% income tax brackets).
- ☐ Perpetual existence—the death or bankruptcy of a shareholder has no effect on the corporate status.

Disadvantages of S Corporations

- ☐ Formation and regulatory requirements are legally complex.

- ☐ S corporations are generally required to use a calendar year-end, thereby negating the income-shifting options of C corporations.

- ☐ Tax liabilities pass to shareholders even if distributions or dividends are not paid.

- ☐ Benefits provided to an employee that is a shareholder are taxable as compensation if he/she owns more than 2% of the S corporation.

- ☐ Shareholder's interests are not freely transferable because S corporations are limited to one class of stock and a maximum of 100 shareholders, each of whom must be either US citizens, resident aliens, estates, or certain qualified trusts. These shareholder restrictions also severely limit access to financing from corporations, partnerships, or limited liability companies.

Personal Service Corporation

State laws prohibit specified professionals—accountants, lawyers, physicians, and others, depending on state statute—from forming C corporations. If these professionals want to incorporate, they must do so as "professional" corporations. Each state licenses and regulates various professions and determines who may, or may not, form a professional corporation. In turn, most professional corporations are classified by the federal tax code as "personal service corporations" (PSCs).[8] Those professional corporations that do not qualify as PSCs are treated as general partnerships for federal taxation purposes.

Qualifying

Professional corporations organized under state law must pass two tests imposed by the IRS to qualify as PSCs. The first, the "function" test, focuses on what the corporation does, and the second, the "ownership" test, measures who owns it. To pass each test a professional corporation must meet a "substantially all" threshold—meaning 95% or more.

Function Test

Substantially all (95 percent or more) of the business activities of the PSC must be personal services that fall within the fields of "health, law, engineering, accounting, architecture, veterinarians, actuarial science, performing arts, or consulting."[9]

Ownership Test

Substantially all (95 percent or more) of the corporation's stock (by value) must be owned directly (or indirectly through one or more partnerships, S corporations, or QPSCs not described in IRC § 448(a)(2) or (3)) by:

1. Employees who are performing services that satisfy the function test on the corporation's behalf (for example, a physician performing medical services);
2. Retired employees who had performed these services on the corporation's behalf;

3. Estates of employees or retired employees who had performed these services on the corporation's behalf; or

4. Other persons who acquired stock from employees or retired employees who had performed services on the corporation's behalf (but only for a two-year period).

Personal Service Corporation (PSC): The tax law does not provide one sole definition of a PSC. Under IRC § 441, a "personal service corporation" is a C corporation whose principal activity is the performance of personal services and whose personal services are substantially performed by employee owners.

Qualified Personal Service Corporation (QPSC): To be a QPSC, a corporation must satisfy both the function test and the ownership test.

Taxation

For tax purposes, a PSC is a separate entity from its owners and it must file its own corporate tax return every year. In theory, a PSC is subject to a flat 35% tax rate on its net income. In practice, the shareholders of PSCs are usually also the employees, and they take out all profits as corporately tax-deductible salaries, bonuses, and fringe benefits. Therefore, a PSC must always file a federal tax return but, seldom ends up paying federal taxes.

Limited Liability Company (LLC)

The limited liability company (LLC) is a hybrid entity that combines the pass-through taxation of a sole proprietorship or partnership with the liability protection that is available through incorporating. The LLC was developed under state laws in the early 1990s in the interest of providing owners with an "ideal" business entity. It was designed to offset the inherent lack of flexibility and the complexity in meeting the eligibility requirements of S corporations.

All 50 states have legislation providing for limited liability companies. However, the laws for each state are somewhat different because "model" or "uniform" laws such as those for corporations and partnerships have not been adopted. As a result, transactions outside the state of formation by the LLC may be treated differently from transactions within the state of formation.

Formation

The specific aspects of forming an LLC vary from state to state; however, every state requires the founders to file Articles of Organization with the office of the secretary of state or another appropriate state office. These articles contain information about the LLC, such as its name, address, purpose, organizers, the registered agent, etc. Some jurisdictions also require that an LLC operating agreement be filed. This document is similar to a partnership agreement since it is the guide for how the business will be conducted. While the LLC formation process is generally very similar to that required to form a corporation, it is generally much less complicated and not as expensive.

Most states have enacted "default" statutes that cover the "fiduciary duties" of LLC owners. These statutes apply only if the founding parties have failed to address a particular item in their LLC operating agreement. Because this regulatory approach allows founders so much latitude, it is important that they draft an operating agreement that is customized for the business that is being conducted and takes full advantage of the flexibility inherent in the LLC structure.

In most states and in most LLC operating agreements, owners are referred to as *members*. Often, the operating agreement will set forth procedures for members to appoint *managers* who are responsible for the day-to-day operations of the LLC.

LLCs can have several different classes of members with varying rights to profits and losses that may be different from their ownership interests in the LLC. For example, a member with 50% ownership interest may be entitled to 65% of LLC losses during the first few years of operations. This may allow that member to reduce his overall tax burden through claiming the LLC losses as offsets against other business income. In addition, LLCs can have an unlimited number of members. LLC owners may be individuals (resident or nonresident), estates, trusts, corporations, partnerships, or other LLCs. These ownership options give LLCs the flexibility to seek a wide range of third-party financing alternatives.

From a management standpoint, unlike general partners or S corporation owners, LLC members may be legally excluded from having a say in running the business. This is allowed as long as the management restrictions are covered in the operating agreement, and the powerless members agree. These members are likely to be investors in the LLC and are similar to limited partners or shareholders with nonvoting equity interests in a corporation.

Liability

Under state law, LLC owners are given the protection from liability that was previously afforded only to corporate shareholders. Generally speaking, owners are not personally liable for the LLC's debts, legal and financial obligations, or losses resulting from lawsuits. However, LLC owners can still be held personally liable for:

- ☐ Debts, if the owner signed a personal guarantee in order to secure a loan;
- ☐ Overdue payroll taxes, especially in small LLCs where the owners have an active part in management;
- ☐ Breaches of fiduciary duty if the owner does not act in the best interests of the LLC and other members; and
- ☐ Owners that use the LLC as an extension of their personal affairs rather than as a separate legal entity.

Some states allow specified professionals to form LLCs—called Limited Liability Partnerships (LLPs) or Limited Liability Limited Partnerships (LLLPs)—as an alternative to personal service corporations. When properly formed, the partners of LLPs or LLLPs receive limited liability protection from the malpractice of the other partners, but remain liable for their own personal acts. The limited liability protection features—not taxes—are the reason that professionals form these types of LLCs.

Taxation

There are two default taxation treatments for LLCs depending on how many members there are in the LLC. For a single member LLC, the LLC will generally be treated as "disregarded" for federal and state tax purposes (i.e. the LLC is ignored and the profits or loss are reported on the member's return). In community property states, a husband and wife are treated as one member. Otherwise, if there are two or more members, an LLC is normally treated as a partnership for both federal and state tax purposes. For federal tax purposes, LLCs must file a Form 1065, *U.S. Partnership Return of Income*. (Single-owner LLCs are exempt from this requirement; they simply file a Schedule C with the owner's Form 1040 like a sole proprietorship.) The LLC does not pay income taxes; therefore, the Form 1065 is an "informational" return that is only used to tell the IRS how much the business earned or lost that year. Instead, LLC profits and losses pass-through the business to its owners. Each owner pays taxes on his share of profit (or deducts his share of losses) on his individual income tax return (Form 1040 with Schedule E attached).

The members of an LLC can choose to have the business taxed like a C corporation rather than as a pass-through entity. While the avoidance of double taxation is of paramount importance to most LLC owners, others might find that they can save taxes by utilizing income-splitting strategies available under C corporation taxation rules. For example, owners of successful LLCs might want to keep some profits in the business at year-end—a tactic that is only available as a C corporation. For this reason, some LLCs start out being taxed as partnerships, and then opt for C corporation taxation when the business is making enough money to justify retaining after-tax earnings, rather than distributing all pre-tax profits to the members under partnership taxation rules.

The members of an LLC can also choose to have the business taxed like an S corporation. This strategy eliminates the double taxation of a C corporation, and also allows the owners to avoid paying self-employment taxes. The owners must take "reasonable compensation" in the form of salary, but this vague requirement allows the owners to take part of the LLC's profits as salary (subject to payroll taxes), and part of the profits as distributions. Each owner pays taxes on his or her share of profit (or deducts his share of losses) on his or her individual income tax return (Form 1040 with Schedule E attached).

Advantages of LLCs

- ☐ Many states allow broad flexibility in structuring LLCs through operating agreements that override "default" regulations that would otherwise govern LLCs. This flexibility makes the LLC an attractive entity for both active management and passive investment ownership objectives.

- ☐ LLCs overcome the ownership restrictions of S corporations while retaining pass-through taxation provisions and liability protection for owners.

- ☐ Owners of an LLC may distribute profits and losses in any manner that they desire without regard to each member's ownership share in the business.

- ☐ LLCs may issue different classes of ownership, do not have limits on the number of members, and may own stock in a C corporation (Single-member LLCs can own stock in S corporations, too.).

- ☐ LLC owners avoid most of the legal complexities and rules found in their state's corporate codes (issuing stock, electing officers, holding meetings, keeping minutes, etc.).

- ☐ Participation in the management affairs of an LLC does not result in the loss of limited liability protection as it does in partnerships.

- ☐ No double taxation—tax liabilities are not assessed at the corporate level unless members specifically opt for C corporate taxation rules.

Disadvantages of LLCs

- ☐ Because the LLC is still a relatively new entity, there is less legal precedent available than traditional business organization law. In addition, the interpretation of the legalities of LLCs varies from state to state. For instance, under various state laws, some LLCs cannot be perpetual and certain types of businesses may not qualify.

- ☐ An LLC usually costs more to form and maintain than a sole proprietorship or general partnership.

- ☐ Tax liabilities pass to members even if there are no distributions from the LLC.

- ☐ In most well-organized, small LLCs, ownership interests will not be freely transferable because of restrictive covenants within their operating agreements. These restrictions are designed to protect LLC owners from having new co-owners forced on them without their approval.

- ☐ States have varying laws regarding the continuity of LLCs. In some states, LLCs dissolve on the death or withdrawal of an owner.

Joint Venture

A joint venture is a temporary business arrangement between two or more legal entities. It is generally designed to carry out a single business transaction or series of related transactions. Because of their limited scope and business-to-business focus, discussion on joint ventures are not covered in this book.

Entity Structuring

> *"In life, as in football, you won't go far unless you know where the goalposts are."*
>
> —Arnold Glasow

Control Issues

Control is one of the most important issues for owners to review when they are determining how they will operate their businesses. The degree of ownership control is defined within state and federal statutes for all business entities except the LLC.

Only one of the legal structures, a sole proprietorship, provides its owner with complete and autonomous control—primarily because, by definition, there is only one owner. A general partner of a limited partnership also has complete control if he or she is the only general partner; otherwise, the general partner of any partnership shares control equally with all of the other general partners.

Corporations are owned by shareholders who appoint the board of directors, which, in turn, appoints officers. Officers have the highest authority over the day-to-day operations of the business. If an S corporation has only one shareholder, that individual also has complete control over the business.

LLCs allow organizers the unique flexibility to set the level of control by owners through covenants within their operating agreements. The owners/members can be divided into categories that have specific and distinctly different levels of management authority. For example, one member/owner may be given complete control over the business and the rest of the members/owners may be limited to a passive investment status. While in another LLC, all members/owners might share in the control of the daily operations—or the operating agreement might be designed so that members/owners appoint managers to fulfill these functions.

Control Issue Comparison

Table 8

Control Issue Comparison

Entity	Control
Sole proprietorship	Owner has complete control over the business.
General partnership	Partners have equal control unless stipulated otherwise by agreement.
Limited partnership	General partners control the business.
C corporation	Officers run day-to-day operations.
S corporation	Same as a C corporation
Limited liability company	Owners have authority and manage as per the operating agreement.

Liability Issues

☑ All of the legal differences between the business entities basically boil down to one issue—personal liability. For startups with one or two owners, this issue may be completely overshadowed by a need to preserve their limited working capital. This is certainly understandable since far more businesses fail financially than those that do not succeed due to a costly lawsuit.

That said, all high-risk endeavors should always insist on limited personal liability for the owners—especially if the business cannot find or afford to purchase appropriate insurance protection. In addition, owners with significant personal assets, businesses with multiple owners, and all passive investors must pay particularly close attention to personal liability issues.

If organizers decide that limiting personal liabilities is worth the extra cost, they have four liability-limiting, business entity choices:

- ☐ Limited partnership
- ☐ C corporation
- ☐ S corporation
- ☐ Limited liability company

These structures (but for the limited partnership) provide liability protection to all of the owners of the business.

With the advent of the LLC, many business owners now opt for this entity over incorporating—unless they need to take advantage of a corporate stock structure to facilitate a public or private financing or to attract key personnel. If this type of corporate stock structure is not required, the simplicity and flexibility offered by LLCs are a clear advantage over corporations. For businesses that never go public, operating as an LLC (rather than as a corporation) typically makes the most sense, provided that limited liability is a primary concern of the founders.

Liability Issue Comparison

Table 9

Liability Issue Comparison

Entity	Liability
Sole proprietorship	Owner is solely liable and his personal assets are at risk.
General partnership	Each partner is "jointly" and "severally" liable for all business debts.
Limited partnership	General partners are responsible for all partnership liabilities. Limited partners are liable up to the amount invested.
C corporation	Shareholders have limited liability up to the amount they invested in stock.
S corporation	Same as a C corporation
Limited liability company	Owners are generally not liable for the debts of the business.

Tax Issues

☑ There are three primary tax issues that affect the selection of a business entity

- ☐ Double taxation
- ☐ The character of pass-through income/losses
- ☐ The deductibility of key expenses

C corporations are the only business entities that face double taxation. Owners of these businesses face two levels of federal taxation:

1. At the corporate level on taxable net profits;
2. At the personal level on distributions or dividend income.

All other forms of doing business are pass-through entities, i.e., owners report their share of business profits or losses in their individual tax returns.

For tax purposes, the character of the pass-through income/loss does not change. Therefore, if a pass-through entity (sole proprietorship, partnership, S corporation, or LLC-as long as it has not elected to be taxed as a C corporation) has a long-term capital gain, the owners must report their proportionate share as a long-term capital gain when they file their individual tax returns.

C corporations are the only legal business entities that:

- ☐ Can retain after-tax earnings
- ☐ Provide owners with income splitting options
- ☐ Can fully deduct the expense of benefits provided to owners/employees

Tax Issue Comparison

Table 10

Tax Issue Comparison

Entity	Federal Taxation
Sole proprietorship	Owner reports all income or loss on his personal tax return.
General partnership	The business pays no tax. Each partner reports his share of income or loss on his personal tax return.
Limited partnership	Same as general partnership.
C corporation	Corporation pays its own taxes and shareholders pay tax on dividends and distributions.
S corporation	Shareholders report their share of income or loss on their personal tax returns. The corporation pays no tax.
Limited liability company	Owners report their share of income or loss on their personal tax returns.

Divide and Conquer

There is a tendency for business owners and their advisors to place all operations in a single business entity. While this may appear at the onset to be the simplest solution, many owners may soon regret this decision. The unlucky ones operate outside the limitations imposed by the business entity they have chosen and are caught. In many of these cases, the difficulties were caused by trying to transact certain aspects of their businesses in the incorrect legal entity. In this scenario, a simple solution becomes an expensive mistake.

☑ On the other hand, tax-wise business owners understand the options available, seek competent legal and financial advice, and are not afraid to strategically divide their business in order to take advantage of key aspects of different legal entities.

For example, it has long been a standard practice in the medical profession for physicians to incorporate as personal service corporations (PSCs), but keep assets such as equipment out of their professional organizations.[10] They set-up the PSC for their medical practice and establish a separate legal entity to own medical equipment or perhaps the building in which they practice.

Why go to this trouble? Because, a PSC does not adequately protect assets from the inherent liabilities of the medical practice, and the use of a separate legal entity solves this limitation while adding other income-splitting options. If the doctor and his or her practice were sued, the assets held by the second organization would be beyond the reach of creditors. In addition, the second entity could charge the PSC a fee to use the equipment or rent to occupy the building. The physician could then transfer income to non-medical service individuals or family members if they owned this entity. The overall tax burden would be reduced since a portion of the doctor's income would be transferred to the owners of the second entity. Taxes on this split income would be paid at the lower income tax rates of these individuals.

The relevant point is that there are advantages and disadvantages to any business structure. Therefore, it often makes sense for owners to divide their activities into multiple entities and thereby conquer the disadvantages of a single business structure. The wealthiest people in the world use this approach to perfection. They do it for a reason—to keep more of what they earn, while protecting what they have, or have been given. It seems to me that this is all the more important if you are not one of the richest people in the world.

☑ Do not "blow off" tax-wise business planning because you do not think that it pertains to you. Remember the old saying: "Those who fail to plan, plan to fail." The rich may be able to afford a failure or two, but the rest of us cannot.

"Money isn't everything as long as you have enough."

—MALCOLM FORBES

Notes

1. Based on the IRS Data books, the audit rates for schedule C filers earning $100,000 is typically four times greater than those of other business entities.
2. This is an allowable deduction for self-employed individuals. (See Schedule SE, Line 6.)
3. There are constant proposals in Congress to eliminate estate taxes (a.k.a. death taxes). I have included the estate tax schedule in the appendix of this book for easy reference.
4. The fiscal year (tax year) of most partnerships is December 31; therefore, the return would be due by midnight on March 15. See IRS Publication 541 for more details.
5. 1986 Tax Reform Act
6. Interstate means activities that cross state lines versus intrastate where activities occur primarily within one jurisdiction. For example, an Internet company whose customers are all over the US would be interstate in nature, while Mom and Pop's Grocery down the street would be intrastate.
7. 1986 Tax Reform Act.
8. IRC §448.
9. Ibid.
10. Doctors and other professionals' corporations fall within the category of a personal service corporation (PSC) and profits are taxed at a flat 35%.

CHAPTER

The Language

"You can't win any game unless you are ready to win."
—Connie Mack

Throughout this book I have presented key terms that have helped to define the language of tax-wise business ownership. This section reviews these terms and introduces several more that are used in Chapter 5 to describe specific business deductions. Understanding these key terms will give business owners the foundation to discuss tax-wise financial matters with their legal and accounting advisors.

Accounting

As discussed in Chapter 3, the business framework that you choose for your enterprise often determines the manner that income is reported and deductions are claimed. In certain cases, business owners may be able to select the income reporting and deduction rules that are best suited for their businesses. And in other cases, the business framework may need to be changed in order to maximize the owner's opportunities to accumulate personal and family wealth.

Fortunately, the IRS provides a detailed discussion of the mechanics of income reporting in Publication 538, *Accounting Periods and Methods*.

Period (Tax Year)

Financial accounting for income and expenses is done on an annual (tax year) basis. Establishing the start and end dates for the accounting period can be by calendar year (January 1 to December 31) or by fiscal year (a 12-month period that ends on any other month except December). However, there are limitations set by the IRS on the use of a fiscal year accounting period.

Certain legal forms for conducting business have a "required year" for accounting purposes, while others do not.

- ☐ S corporations and sole proprietorships are required to use a calendar year for accounting of income and deductions.
- ☐ Partnerships or limited liability companies that are owned by individuals are generally required to use a calendar year, unless the owners can satisfactorily show the IRS that there are valid business reasons for a fiscal year accounting period election.
- ☐ C corporations and certain personal service corporations may elect either a calendar or a fiscal tax year—depending on which reporting period is the most advantageous for their owners.

Within these limitations, business owners may select the tax year without the approval of the IRS. However, a business that wants to change its tax year must first obtain IRS approval. This often involves the filing of Form 8716, *Election to Have a Tax Year Other Than a Required Tax Year*. In general, such a change should be taken under the advice and guidance of your accounting and legal advisors since it often complicates taxation matters.

Methods

There are two principal methods of business accounting:

1. Cash basis method
2. Accrual basis method

The primary difference between these two methods is the way that businesses are allowed to record expenses and claim deductions on their year-end tax returns (i.e., how and when these items are recorded or claimed).

Cash Basis

Under the cash basis method of accounting, expenses are recorded when paid and deductions are allowed for those qualifying expenses that were recorded during the tax year. This means that the unpaid portion of purchases, which were made on credit, do not show up on the accounting ledgers of a cash basis business. Therefore, these expenses are not deducted on the year-end tax return.

Similarly, a business usually cannot deduct prepaid expenses that do not relate to the current tax year. However, tax courts have allowed some taxpayers to deduct prepaid rents and advance payments for insurance premiums. For further clarification, talk with your accountant and tax advisors.

The cash basis is the simplest method of accounting. However, it cannot be used by C corporations, partnerships that have a corporation as a partner, or by business organizations that maintain inventories—unless they are "small businesses." This "small business exception" applies to businesses with average annual gross receipts of $5 million or less in at least one of the three previous tax years.

Accrual Basis

The accrual method of accounting requires a business to deduct expenses when they occur rather than when they are paid.

Except for certain real property taxes and recurring items, the expense "occurs" once all of the following events have happened:

- ☐ All actions necessary to establish a liability have been completed
- ☐ The amount of liability has been reasonably determined
- ☐ Economic performance has occurred (goods or services have been exchanged)

Assets

Business Assets

A business asset is something bought, acquired, or developed that has (or is expected to have) monetary value—and which is used in a business for more than one year. Examples of assets are land, equipment, patents, buildings, and franchise rights. If a taxpayer wishes to deduct the cost of a business asset that cost has to be spread out and deducted over a period of years (amortized or depreciated).

Capital Assets

Capital assets generally include everything that a taxpayer (an individual or a business) owns for use or as an investment—except for depreciable property or business inventories. Examples for individuals are homes, autos, and investment securities (stocks and bonds).

A capital business asset is a property that is used by the business rather than resold to clients or customers. Typically, for federal tax purposes, property that is held by a business is a capital asset—except in the following cases:

- ☐ Property held primarily for resale to customers in the ordinary course of the trade or business;
- ☐ Property used in the trade or business which can be depreciated or certain real property used in the trade or business;
- ☐ Copyrights, literary materials, musical compositions, or other artistic compositions, letters or memoranda, or other similar property held by the business;
- ☐ Accounts or notes receivable acquired in the ordinary course of the trade or business.

Nonbusiness Assets

A nonbusiness asset is a property that is used for personal purposes, such as a home, family car, motor home, or boat.

Real Property

Land and generally anything erected on, growing on, or attached to land are classified as real property—for example, a building.

Fair Market Value (FMV)

Fair market value (FMV) is the price at which an asset would change hands between a buyer and a seller, neither having to buy or sell, and both having reasonable knowledge of all necessary facts about the transaction. (See IRS Publication 551, *Basis of Assets*.)

Basis

Basis or tax basis is a term defined in the U.S. Tax Code. (See IRS Publication 551, *Basis of Assets*.) It is the financial value or starting point for calculating depreciation, amortization, gain, loss, depletion, and casualty losses. From a taxation perspective, basis is the amount that the Code says has been invested in an asset. That amount may be quite different from the value that owners place on these items.

Cost Basis

As a general rule, when equipment is purchased, the beginning tax basis is its original cost, including freight, assembly, and installation (IRC §1012). Basis also includes all applicable state and local taxes. These taxes are deductible along with the item itself; however, sales tax on a capital asset cannot be completely written off in the year that the item is purchased, unless the asset is expensed under IRC §179.

Example

A 6% state sales tax on a trailer that was purchased for $12,000, i.e. $720, is added to the cost to establish the basis in the trailer ($12,720). This basis is then used to calculate the write-off allowed over the period that the trailer is depreciated.

In the case of real property, the basis includes certain fees and other expenses that become a part of the taxpayer's cost basis in the property. In addition, if the real property includes a building, the owner must allocate the basis of the property between the land and the building. This is required in order for the owner to calculate the allowable depreciation of the building since land is never depreciable. There are other special rules for real property that are found in IRS Publication 551, *Basis of Assets*.

Gift (Transferred) Basis

Under IRC §1015, the recipient of a gift of property takes on the same tax basis as the prior owner. This is referred to as the transferred basis in the property. It is important to note that the original holding period for the property is also transferred to the recipient for determination of long-term or short-term capital gains on the sale or disposition of the asset.

Example

John's father-in-law, Pete, gave him industrial real estate in which Pete had a basis in the land of $50,000 and a basis in the warehouse of $50,000. The FMV of the property at the time of the gift was $300,000. John received a $100,000 transferred basis in the property plus any gift tax that Pete may have paid.

If John immediately sold the property for FMV, he would have a capital gain of $200,000. If he then purchased a new business property for $300,000 and allocated 20% of the purchase price to the land ($60,000) and 80% to the building ($240,000), John could depreciate the $240,000 cost basis of the new building.

On the other hand, if John uses the property in his business, he can only depreciate the transferred basis in the building ($50,000). It is important to note that Joe *cannot* step up the basis in the building to its FMV at the date it was transferred to business use. (See "Converted Basis.")

Bartered Basis

Property received in exchange for services has a basis equal to its FMV (IRC §7701 and Publication 551). The basis is treated as barter income to the recipient. Thus, the entire amount is taxable in the year it is received.

Example
Phil is facing a labor dispute in his furniture manufacturing plant and contacts his lawyer, Alex. Phil explains the situation and Alex offers to provide his legal services in exchange for new waiting room furniture for his office. By the time that the dispute has been settled, Alex has provided 20 hours of legal

services. Rather than bill Phil his usual $5,000 fee (20 hours at $250 per hour), Alex accepts waiting room furnishings with a FMV of $10,000 from Phil.

As a result of this barter transaction, Alex should report $10,000 of income, but he will be able to depreciate the furniture and might be able to expense the entire amount under IRC §179. Phil will show an expense item for legal services that is equal to the cost required to manufacture the furniture.

Inherited Basis

Inherited property, which is subsequently used by the heirs of a business, has a basis that is equal to its FMV at the time of death of the decedent. In essence, the basis in the property is stepped up to the FMV at the date of death (IRC §1014).

> *Example*
>
> Pete bequeaths Joe, his son-in-law, industrial real estate in which Pete had a basis in the land of $50,000 and a basis in the warehouse of $50,000. The FMV of the property at the time of Pete's death was $300,000. Joe's inherited basis is $300,000.
>
> If a FMV of the property at the time of Pete's death would have allocated 20% of the value to the land ($60,000) and 80% to the building ($240,000), Joe could depreciate the $240,000 inherited basis of the building in his business.

Exchanged (Substituted) Basis

If allowed by the Code, when one property is exchanged for another, the recipient's "substituted" basis in the acquired property is equal to the basis in the property that he transferred. Nontaxable transfers of this type are only allowed if the trade is made for a "like-kind" property, i.e. with the same nature or character. (See IRS Publication 544, *Sales and Other Dispositions of Assets*.) For instance, intangible property such as a copyright cannot be exchanged for an automobile. In this case, the attempted exchange would be considered a sale of each item—resulting in a taxable profit or loss to the respective owner.

In addition to the requirement to exchange like-kind properties in order to qualify as a nontaxable exchange, a taxpayer must also hold both the property that is transferred and the one that is received for business or investment purposes.

Example

Pete has a $100,000 basis in an industrial property with a FMV of $300,000. He locates another property that he wants to acquire through a like-kind exchange. After the exchange is completed, Pete would have his same substituted basis ($100,000) in the acquired property.

For clarification on exchanges involving property plus cash, transfers between related persons, partially nontaxable transactions, and partial business use of property, see IRS Publication 544, *Sales and Other Dispositions of Assets*.

Converted Basis

Converted properties are personal items that are either transferred to a business use or are used to produce rent. Under IRC §167, the tax basis of an item that is converted to business use is the lessor of:

- ☐ The FMV on the date of conversion, or
- ☐ The owner's adjusted basis in the property.

Example

Several years ago, Harry paid $350,000 for a sport fishing boat for his personal use. In the intervening years Harry paid $50,000 to upgrade the interior, engines, and navigational systems. Now that Harry is retiring from his medical practice, he decides to pursue his dream of running a sport fishing charter service. Harry forms his company, Dream Line Enterprises, LLC, and converts his boat to business use. At the time that the business is started, Harry receives an appraisal that values the boat at $475,000 FMV. Through Dream Line Enterprises, LLC Harry can depreciate $400,000 (his adjusted basis in the boat).

Adjusted Basis

An owner must usually make adjustment to the basis of a property before he can calculate:

- ☐ The gain or loss on a sale, exchange, or other disposition of property
- ☐ Allowable depreciation, depletion, or amortization

Increases to Basis

Uniform Capitalization Rules

The uniform capitalization rules (found in IRS Publication 551, *Basis of Assets*, and IRS Publication 538, *Accounting Periods and Methods*) specify the costs that certain owners must add to the basis of business assets. These rules apply to businesses that:

- ☐ Produce tangible property for use in a business or for sale to customers
- ☐ Acquire property for resale

Production means the building, installing, manufacturing, developing, improving, creating, raising, or growing of the property.

Under these rules, owners must capitalize all direct costs as well as a portion of indirect costs incurred in their production or resale activities. This means that these expenses must be added to the basis of the produced or acquired properties rather than deducted as current expenses. These costs are then written off through depreciation, amortization, or cost of goods sold when the properties are used, sold, or otherwise disposed.

Real Estate

The cost of any improvement that has a useful life of more than one year is added to the basis of real property. These include amounts spent to prolong the life of the property, increase its value, or adapt it to a different use. In addition, the following are examples of costs that increase basis:

- ☐ Extending utility service lines
- ☐ Legal fees for perfecting or protecting title, etc.
- ☐ Zoning costs
- ☐ Rehabilitation expenses (minus rehabilitation credits received, if any)
- ☐ Assessments for items that increase the value of the property such as paving roads

Deducting Versus Capitalizing Costs

The primary rule is that items that can be deducted as current expenses cannot be added to the basis of an asset.

Example

The amounts paid for the repair and maintenance of a business vehicle are deductible as a business expense. Therefore, these expenses cannot be added to the vehicle's basis.

However, specific costs can be deducted as a current expense or capitalized (added to the basis) and then depreciated, amortized, or depleted. These include:

- ☐ Carrying charges on property (e.g., interest and taxes) except those required to be capitalized under the uniform capitalization rules
- ☐ Research and experimentation costs
- ☐ Intangible drilling and development costs for oil, gas, and geothermal wells

- ☐ Exploration costs for new mineral deposits
- ☐ Newspaper or periodical circulation costs
- ☐ Remodeling cost to remove barriers for people with disabilities and the elderly

Decreases to Basis

The following are some of the items that reduce the basis of a business property:

- ☐ Section 179 deductions
- ☐ Deductions previously allowed for depreciation, amortization, or depletion
- ☐ Nontaxable corporate distributions
- ☐ Casualty and theft losses and insurance reimbursements
- ☐ Any investment credit, disabled access credit, or enhanced oil recovery credit taken
- ☐ Certain canceled debt excluded from income
- ☐ Rebates received from a manufacturer or seller

Deducting Expenses

Capital Expenses

Capital expenses are costs that are added to (increase) the basis of a taxpayer's capital asset (investment or non-depreciable property).

Deductible Expenses

Any product or service purchased for use by (or in) a business is deductible if it is "ordinary and reasonable" for that type of business. For tax purposes, a deductible expense is money a business pays for products or services that are used within the current year. For cash-basis taxpayers, these costs are deductible in the year they are incurred.

Nondeductible Expenses

The cost of capital assets as well as the cost of intangible property that does not have a defined useful life cannot be written off. The following are examples of items that cannot be deducted or that can be deducted under certain limited circumstances:

- ☐ Land—Land can never be depreciated; however, if it is used for mining or logging, it can be depleted. In addition, clearing, grading, and landscaping expenses are usually added to the basis of the land rather than depreciated.
- ☐ Trademarks and trade names
- ☐ Goodwill—Goodwill is not depreciable; however, customer lists, subscriber lists, etc. are depreciable if their values are separated from that of goodwill.
- ☐ Franchises, designs, drawings, and patterns—These items are deductible only if a useful life can be determined.

Deductibility of an expense will often depend on how a business transaction is set up. Tax-wise business owners should consult their legal and financial advisors before spending any substantial sums on capital assets or intangible property.

Timing

☑ Most deductions are taken in the year that they are either paid or incurred, depending upon which method of accounting is used. However, there are many exceptions to this rule. For instance, some prepaid expenses (property taxes and interest on debts) must be deducted in the tax year for which they apply. Other expenses must be written off (depreciated) over a period of years (e.g., autos and office equipment); but goods offered for sale (from the business' shelve stocks or inventory) cannot be written off until they are sold.

Depreciation

Depreciation is a special type of business deduction that allows a business owner to deduct a portion of the cost of equipment or property used in a business. It is an annual income tax deduction that allows the business owner to recover the basis of certain property over the time that the property is in use (the useful life of the asset). Sometimes depreciation can be structured so that the majority of the write-off is taken in the first few years of ownership.

The financial concept behind depreciation is that business equipment wears out over time and must, therefore, be replaced periodically. In theory, the cumulative total of the allowed depreciation would be sufficient to purchase a replacement asset. This is not likely, but it is still a valid theory.

Except for those items that the taxpayer elects to expense in the first year (See "Section 179 Deductions"), tangible business property (i.e., things you can see or touch) with a useful life of more than one year must be depreciated.

Calculating a depreciation allowance is a complex process. It involves:

- ☐ Researching the class life of the property;
- ☐ Selecting one of the two depreciation systems;
- ☐ Applying one of the four authorized depreciation methods.

Appendix B of IRS Publication 946, *How to Depreciate Property*, and IRC §168, *Accelerated Cost Recovery System*, list the class lives of assets as well as their respective recovery periods under the two depreciation systems.

Class Life

Every kind of asset is assigned a class life. It is used to identify the property class of the asset and the minimum time period (recovery period) over which its basis can be deducted.

General Depreciation System (GDS)

Under the general depreciation system (GDS), property is depreciated over one of the following recovery periods.

Property Class	Recovery Period
3-year property	3 years
5-year property	5 years
7-year property	7 years
10-year property	10 years
15-year property	15 years
20-year property	20 years
25-year property	25 years
Residential rental property	27.5 years
Nonresidential real property	39 years

Most business assets fall into one of the following property classes under the GDS:

- ☐ *3-year property*
  Examples: equipment used in manufacturing plastics, metal fabrication, and glass.
- ☐ *5-year property*
  Examples: aircraft; cars; office equipment; computers and peripherals; and equipment used for apparel manufacturing, construction, research, and experimentation.
- ☐ *7-year property*
  Examples: office furniture and fixtures; agricultural structures; and oil, gas, and mining assets.

☐ *Nonresidential real property*
Business real estate (except land which is never depreciated) has a recovery period of 39 years. Specifically identified land improvement costs (landscaping, roads, etc.) are depreciable over 15 years.

Alternative Depreciation System (ADS)

For most property, the recovery periods are generally longer under the alternative depreciation system (ADS) than they are under the GDS. The following table shows some of the ADS recovery periods.

Table 11

ADS Recovery Periods

Property	Recovery Period
Rent-to-own property	4 years
Automobiles and light duty trucks	5 years
Computers and peripheral equipment	5 years
High technology medical equipment	5 years
Personal property with no class life	12 years
Single purpose agricultural structures	15 years
Nonresidential real property	40 years

Depreciation Methods

The IRC provides three depreciation methods under GDS and one depreciation method under ADS.

☐ The 200% declining balance method over a GDS recovery period.

☐ The 150% declining balance method over a GDS recovery period.

☐ The straight line method over a GDS or ADS recovery period.

Comparisons

The following table compares the benefits that business owners receive by using different depreciation methods for various types of properties.

Table 12

Depreciation Comparison

Method	Type of Property	Benefit
GDS using 200% declining balance	• Nonfarm 3-, 5-, 7-, and 10-year property	• Provides a greater deduction during earlier recovery years. • Changes to straight line when that method provides an equal or greater deduction.
GDS using 150% declining balance	• All farm property (except real property) • All 15- and 20-year property • Nonfarm 3-, 5-, 7-, and 10-year property	• Provides a greater deduction during the earlier recovery years. • Changes to straight line when that method provides an equal or greater deduction.

GDS using straight line	• Nonresidential real property • Residential rental property • All 3-, 5-, 7-, and 10-year property	• Provides for equal yearly deductions (except for the first and last years).
ADS using straight line	• Listed property used 50% or less for business • Property used predominantly outside the U.S. • Qualified leasehold improvement property placed in service before January 1, 2014 • Qualified restaurant property placed in service before January 1, 2014 • Tax-exempt property • Farm property used when an election not to apply the uniform capitalization rules is in effect • Imported property • Any property for which you elect to use this method	• Provides for equal yearly deductions.

Section 179 Deductions

Section 179 of the Code allows taxpayers to write off certain equipment costs in one year instead of spreading them out (depreciating them) over time. To take this deduction a taxpayer must:

- ☐ Be able to prove that the equipment is used more than 50% of the time for business;
- ☐ Prorate the cost to his business usage, i.e., if he uses it 60% of the time for business, he can expense 60% of the cost;
- ☐ Recapture (pay back) a portion of the deduction if he disposes of the property or stops using it for business purposes before the end of its useful life.

Special restrictions also apply to motor vehicles. For 2014, no more than $3,160 of a new car's cost can be deducted as a Section 179 deduction if you elected not to claim any special depreciation allowance or the vehicle is not qualified property.

The Section 179 equipment write-off is limited to a maximum of $500,000 for 2015 and beyond). The $500,000 limit is per taxpayer, not per business. Thus, if a taxpayer has more than one business, the maximum he can expense for 2015 under Section 179 is $500,000. Married individuals filing separate returns are treated as one taxpayer with a combined limit of $500,000. However, if more than $2,000,000 of equipment is purchased in the year, the amount that may be expensed is reduced by one dollar for each dollar over $2,000,000 in 2015 and beyond).

Bonus Depreciation

Since 2008, taxpayers have been able to immediately expense more of the purchase price of certain assets due to "bonus depreciation" under Section 168 of the Code. In most years, bonus depreciation allows for the immediate expensing of 50% of the adjusted basis of qualifying property. Bonus depreciation is only allowed on new assets; used assets do not qualify.

The year-end fiscal cliff deals in 2012 and 2013 and 2015 brought the 50% bonus depreciation back, allowing the option to immediately deduct half the cost of qualifying assets in the year of acquisition, plus the regular, year-one depreciation on the remaining basis.

REV. PROC. 2013-21 TABLE 1	
DEPRECIATION LIMITATIONS FOR PASSENGER AUTOMOBILES (THAT ARE NOT TRUCKS OR VANS) PLACED IN SERVICE IN CALENDAR YEAR 2013 FOR WHICH THE § 168(k) ADDITIONAL FIRST YEAR DEPRECIATION DEDUCTION APPLIES	
Tax Year	Amount
1st Tax Year	$11,160
2nd Tax Year	$ 5,100
3rd Tax Year	$ 3,050
Each Succeeding Year	$ 1,875

REV. PROC. 2013-21 TABLE 2	
DEPRECIATION LIMITATIONS FOR TRUCKS AND VANS PLACED IN SERVICE IN CALENDAR YEAR 2013 FOR WHICH THE § 168(k) ADDITIONAL FIRST YEAR DEPRECIATION DEDUCTION APPLIES	
Tax Year	Amount
1st Tax Year	$11,360
2nd Tax Year	$ 5,400
3rd Tax Year	$ 3,250
Each Succeeding Year	$ 1,975

The IRS gave special treatment in Revenue Procedure 2003-75, for "trucks and vans," which were allowed higher depreciation limits. A truck or van generally means any passenger auto—including an SUV— that is built on a truck chassis with a loaded gross weight of no more than 6,000 pounds. Revenue

Procedure 2013–21 set out new depreciation limits for trucks and vans (see table below).

The IRS issued Revenue Procedure 2013–21, which sets the annual depreciation limits for luxury autos. If you elect to apply the bonus depreciation rules to a newly-purchased auto, instead of getting a total year-one deduction equal to 60% of your purchase price, you are limited under Section 280F to a maximum deduction of $11,160.

$20,000	MACRS Depreciation	Section 280F Limit	Allowable Depreciation
Year 1	$12,000	$11,160	$11,160
Year 2	$3,200	$5,100	$3,200
Year 3	$1,920	$1,875	$1,875
Year 4	$1,150	$1,875	$1,150
Year 5	$1,150	$1,875	$1,150
Year 6	$580	$1,875	$580

Amortization

Amortization is also an incrementally applied deduction that is conceptually similar to depreciation. Amortization of a capitalized asset must be specifically allowed by the Code. (See IRC Publication 535, *Business Expenses*.) Many of these allowances are for intangible assets (IRC §197 intangibles) that are acquired in the purchase of a business, such as:

- ☐ Goodwill
- ☐ Going concern and workforce values
- ☐ Intellectual property—patents, copyrights, etc.
- ☐ Governmentally granted rights—licenses, permits, etc.
- ☐ Brand value—franchises, trademarks, etc.

In addition, a business may elect to amortize certain types of expenditures that would not otherwise be deductible, such as:

- ☐ Organizational expenses
- ☐ Start-up costs
- ☐ Costs acquiring a lease
- ☐ Interest and taxes paid during construction
- ☐ Pollution control facilities

As a general rule, the basis of capitalized assets that have to be amortized will be spread out over a longer time period than those that are depreciated.

Depletion

Depletion is a yearly deduction that allows a taxpayer to recover an investment in mineral resources (that are in place) or in standing timber properties. In order to claim this deduction the taxpayer must have the right to income from either the extraction and sale of the minerals or from the cutting of the timber.

Date of Service

The date of service is the date that an asset is ready and available for a specific use, whether or not it is actually in use on that date.

Useful Life

IRS Publication 946, *How to Depreciate Property*, provides taxpayers with the allowable useful life of various classifications of depreciable business assets.

Deduction Categories

In general, allowable deductions fall into three broad categories:

- ☐ Current Expenses—deductible in the year incurred
- ☐ Depreciable Assets—alternatively expensed under IRC §179
- ☐ Amortizable Costs

From a tax standpoint, an allowable deduction from any of these categories provides a tax deduction—i.e., a dollar amount that is subtracted from total business income (gross sales / fees) in order to arrive at taxable income (net profit).

Computing taxable business income is a multi-step process.

1. The first task is to compute "gross profit." Gross profit is gross income reduced by:

    - ☐ Refunds made to customers

☐ The cost of inventory sold during the year, i.e., cost of goods sold

Note: Businesses cannot deduct the cost of inventory until the goods are sold.

2. Gross profit is then reduced by all other allowable business deductions to arrive at the net taxable profits of the business.

Current Expenses

For cash-basis taxpayers, current expenses—the everyday costs of keeping a business going—are deductible in the year they are incurred. The rules for deducting a current expense are straight forward, i.e., subtract it from profits in the year it occurs. However, some expenses have special rules that govern how and to what extent they are deductible—business meals and vehicle expenses, for example. In addition, the legal form of the business may impose a limitation (or allow more of a deduction) for some current expenses.

Table 13
Examples of Current Expenses
(Deductible in the Year Incurred)

Accident & Health Benefits	Accounting & Bookkeeping
Achievement Awards	Adoption Assistance
Advertising	Appraisals
Assessments	Associations—Clubs
Athletic Facilities	Attorney Fees
Bad Debts	Bank Fees
Bartering	Bonuses
Charitable Contributions	Cleaning Services
Communication Fees	Conventions
Credit Cards	De Minimis (Minimal) Benefits
Dependent Care	Deposits
Directors' Fees	Dividends
Education	Employees' Pay
Entertainment	Fringe Benefits
Home Office	Independent Contractors
Insurance	Interest
Internet	Licenses
Leases	Meals
Office Services	Postage
Product Development	Promotion
Property Improvements	Publications
Reimbursements	Rent
Repairs	Royalties
Seminars	Shipping and Freight
Supplies	Tax Credits
Taxes	Travel
Vehicle Expenses	Utilities

Depreciable Assets

Depreciation is an annual income tax deduction that allows a business to recover the cost or other basis of certain property over the time the property is used. It is an allowance for the wear and tear, age, deterioration, or obsolescence of the property.

☑ Section 179 of the code allows taxpayers to write off the cost of certain equipment in the year purchased instead of depreciating the cost over the time it is used. For the year 2015, the write-off is limited to a maximum of $500,000, or net income, whichever is lower. However, if more than $2,000,000 of equipment is purchased in the year, the amount that may be expensed is reduced by one dollar for each dollar over $2,000,000 ($500,000 in 2015 with inflation adjustments for future years). In other words, if the cost of your qualifying section 179 property placed in service in 2015 is over $2,000,000, you must reduce the dollar limit (but not below zero) by the amount of cost over $2,000,000.

If the cost of your section 179 property placed in service during the year is $2,500,000 or more, you cannot take a section 179 expense deduction and you cannot carry over the cost that is more than $2,500,000.

(See IRS Publication 946, *How To Depreciate Property*, and Chapter 4, Basis, Depreciation, and Section 179 Deductions.)

Table 14
Examples of Assets to Depreciate
or Expense Under Section 179

Athletic Facilities	Communications Equipment
Computer Software	Computers and Peripherals
Furniture and Fixtures	Information Systems
Office Equipment	Product Development
Production Equipment	Property Improvements
Real Estate (except land)	Shipping and Freight
Tools	Vehicles

Amortizable Costs

Amortization is a method of recovering (deducting) capital costs over a fixed period of time. It is similar to the straight-line method of depreciation in that costs are deducted in equal amounts over the period of amortization. The actual deduction amount is found by dividing the allowed costs by the months in the amortization period. The result is the amount that a taxpayer can deduct for each month.

☑ Within the guidelines set in IRS Publication 535, *Business Expenses*, business owners are sometimes allowed to choose a period for amortizing certain costs. Once an amortization period is selected, it cannot be changed. (See IRS Publication 946, *How To Depreciate Property*.)

Amortization that begins during the current year is deducted by completing Part VI of Form 4562, *Depreciation and Amortization*. Unless a Form 4562 is subsequently required for the years following the year that amortization began, amortization is claimed directly on the "Other expenses" line of schedule C or F (Form 1040) or the "Other deductions" line of Form 1065, Form 1120, Form 1120-A, or Form 1120-S.

Table 15
Examples of Amortizable Costs

Reforestation costs	Business Set Up Expenses
Intellectual Property	Leases
Product Development	Geological and geophysical costs
Costs of research and experimentation	Section 197 Intangibles
Costs of certain tax preferences	Costs of pollution control facilities

Deducting Limitations

☑ As discussed in Chapter 3, all deductions are not handled uniformly. In fact, when cumulative expenses exceed the income generated by the business, there are three important rules that determine whether deductions will be partially allowed, delayed, or entirely disallowed.

☐ Hobby Loss Rules (See IRS Publication 535, *Business Expenses*.)

- ☐ Passive Activity Rules (See IRS Publication 925, *Passive Activity and At-Risk Rules*.)
- ☐ At-Risk Rules (See IRS Publication 925, *Passive Activity and At-Risk Rules*.)

Hobby Loss Rules

☑ The IRS presumes that a business is engaged in activities "for profit"—when gross income exceeds expense deductions for three out of five consecutive taxable years (two out of seven consecutive taxable years for breeding, training, showing, or racing horses). If a business fails to meet these income parameters, the IRS may classify it as a hobby (except as noted later in this chapter). When this happens, under IRC Section 183, business losses cannot be claimed in excess of the income generated from the activity (hobby)—unless the owner can successfully argue that the business has a profit motive despite recurrent losses.

Demonstrating a Profit Motive

A business may sustain losses year after year and not be classified as a hobby—provided that it can show that it has made a sufficient effort to make a profit (the burden of proof is on the owner/taxpayer). There are no hard and fast ways to prove a profit motive—but there are several guidelines that owners can use to demonstrate this intent.

Work in a Businesslike Manner

Operate the business by keeping appropriate records, separate personal assets and finances from those of the business, and establish a business presence (bank account, telephone, stationery, etc.).

Commit Sufficient Time and Effort

Spend enough time and effort to show that you could realistically expect to make a profit.

Have the Prerequisite Expertise

Personally have, or hire personnel with, the expertise to successfully run the business.

Seek Advice

Obtain the counsel of experts to improve the operation of the business.

Analyze the Financial History

Document business losses incurred in the startup phase as well as any losses from unforeseen circumstances. In addition, a for-profit motive may be established if historic, but occasional, profits are large when compared with the owner's investment and the losses suffered.

Identify Appreciating Assets

Provide data that supports the likelihood that business assets will appreciate in value and thereby generate future profits on gains from their sale— even though the business currently operates at a loss.

Demonstrate a Dependence on the Income

The more reliant the owner is on the business as a primary source of income, the more he or she shows a for-profit motive. This reliance is often best shown by identifying the employment and/or income that the owner has forfeited in order to focus on the business.

✓ *Note:* The determination of whether there is a profit motive is made at the business level, rather than at the owner level, because losses pass through the business to the owner. In other words, the business must reasonably expect to make a profit, regardless of an owner's intent. A hobby loss cannot be claimed as a deductible loss at the owner level, unless the business itself demonstrates a profit motive.

Effect of Business Structure

Hobby loss rules do not apply to businesses that file tax returns under Subchapter C of the Code, i.e.,

- ☐ C corporations
- ☐ Personal service corporations
- ☐ LLCs that have elected to be taxed under Subchapter C of the Code
- ☐ Hobby loss rules apply to:
- ☐ Sole proprietorships
- ☐ Partnerships (general and limited)
- ☐ The majority of limited liability companies
- ☐ S corporations

Sole proprietorships, partnerships, LLCs, or S corporations that may otherwise be subject to the hobby loss rules are exempt from hobby loss limitations if they have:

- ☐ Met the for-profit income parameters; or
- ☐ Demonstrated a for-profit motive

Since these business forms are pass-through entities, each owner may claim his or her pro rata share of business deductions up to the amount of his income from *all activities*. Excess losses, if any, are carried over into the following tax years.

On the other hand, when a business is subject to hobby loss limitations, losses deducted at the owner level are limited to the extent of the income produced by that hobby. Therefore, hobby losses <u>cannot</u> be claimed against income from other sources. (Some expenses such as taxes, interest, and casualty losses are deductible regardless of the hobby income limitation.)

Compliance Strategies

Short-Term Profitability

A business, with alternating profitable and unprofitable years, may be able to qualify for the presumption of a profit motive by timing profit and loss recognition. Through proper management, the business may be able to focus on purchases that generate deductions in "loss" years and then maximize income and minimize deductions in three consecutive "profit" years.

Long-Term Profitability

Businesses that will not be profitable for a number of years will not be able to establish a for-profit motive through the timing of deductions and income. These firms will need to demonstrate a for-profit motive by meeting several of the guidelines discussed earlier.

No Profitability

If a business has no possibility of ever making a profit, the owners have two choices. Obviously, they can accept the fact that they are running a hobby and follow the income declaration and hobby loss limitations imposed by these rules. Alternatively, the business owners can reorganize the business so that it is taxed under Subchapter C of the Code (e.g., C corporation or electing LLC).

Passive Activity Rules

☑ The passive activity rules apply to business relationships where the owners do not "materially participate," as well as any business activity that involves the rental of real property. The Code sets forth seven tests to determine the material participation of a business owner. Passing any one of these tests demonstrates to the IRS that the owner's interest in the income and losses generated by the business is not subject to the limitations imposed by the passive activity rules.

Material Participation Tests

> To pass the basic material participation test, an owner must participate in the business for a minimum of 500 hours per year—regardless of the number of other participants.
>
> An owner passes if he or she is the only participant in the business—this limitation includes non-owner individuals.

An owner passes the test if he or she participates at least 100 hours per year, and if that participation is at least as much as any other individual involved in the business (owners and non-owners).

If the business is a "significant participation activity" (i.e., one that requires more than 500 hours of participation per year), an owner qualifies as a material participant if he or she participates more than 100 hours per year and does not qualify under any of the other tests.

An owner passes the test if he or she has materially participated in the business for any five of the 10 preceding years (consecutive or non-consecutive years).

An owner of personal service businesses passes the test if he or she has materially participated for any of the three preceding tax years (consecutive or non-consecutive years).

An owner who can demonstrate that he or she has participated in a business on a "regular, continuous, and substantial basis" for more than 100 hours in a tax year pass the material participation test. However, managing activities are not counted if the business compensates others to manage or if any other individual spends more time managing than the owner (paid or unpaid).

Taxation

Except under restricted conditions in the area of passive real estate rental income, the Code limits deduction of losses from passive activities to the amount of the taxpayer's passive income from all sources. All excess passive losses are carried forward to following years and/or until the property is sold. However, all of the taxpayer's net passive income is taxable in the year it is received.

At-Risk Rules

Not long ago, businesses were frequently funded through a combination of a small sum of cash and a large note for which the funding party had no personal liability. The object was to raise the investor's "basis" in the business investment in order to increase the amount of tax write-offs that could be claimed if the business failed. If this happened, the funding investor could claim deductions that were larger than the cash actually invested in the business. Congress created the at-risk rules to abolish these practices.

In a nutshell, when they apply, the at-risk rules limit an owner's deductible losses to the amount that he or she has at risk (i.e., the amount that he or she could potentially lose if the business fails). Thus, losses are limited to the amounts that are actually at risk in the business (e.g., the cash, adjusted basis of contributed assets, and debts that are secured by other assets or personal guarantees). These items form the at-risk basis—the limit to which losses can be claimed. The at-risk basis is calculated at the end of each tax year. Losses that are allowed reduce the basis, but losses that exceed the basis in a tax year cannot be claimed. These excess losses are carried over to be used in subsequent years. Upon the sale of the investment, the gain can be offset by the amount of the carried-over losses.

☑ Your legal and tax advisors can guide you through the at-risk rules. But, as a practical matter, owners who set up and conduct active businesses generally do not have to worry about at-risk rules. In addition, certain types of investments such as those in closely held C corporations are exempt from the at-risk rules if the business meets the active business tests and does not engage in equipment leasing or activities involving audio, visual, artistic, or literary property.

Record Keeping

General Guidelines

As a general rule—and there are many exceptions—the IRS has three years after a return is filed to conduct an audit. However, some tax professionals advise keeping all tax forms and supporting records until the statute of limitations expires for IRS audits associated with income underreporting of more than 25%, i.e., six years.

There is no statute of limitation for failure to file a return or filing a fraudulent one. Therefore, if you do not earn enough to file a return, you should retain all records for that year permanently. You will need them to support your nonfiling if, or when, the IRS decides to conduct an audit.

In addition, conservative advisors often recommend that their clients keep all tax-related records for those years in which they claimed exceptionally large deductions. The reason behind this advice is twofold. First, the abnormal jump in deductions may trigger an audit. And, most importantly, these records will be necessary to defend against any IRS allegations of tax fraud.

Expense Records

You cannot deduct expenses unless they are legitimate. Therefore, it stands to reason that business owners must keep meticulous records of each business expense. These records should include the "who, what, when, where, why, and how" of each transaction.

Who incurred the expense and/or who (third parties) benefited (especially for travel and entertainment expenses)?

- ☐ What was purchased?
- ☐ When was the transaction conducted?
- ☐ Where did the business take place?
- ☐ Why was the transaction business-related?
- ☐ How was payment completed?

The most basic record of an expense is a canceled check, electronic funds transfer data, signed receipt, or some other form of proof of payment. Keep all proof-of-payment records that support deductions that are claimed on a tax return. However, proof-of-payment records alone do not mean that the expenses are allowable tax deductions. Therefore, taxpayers must also keep documents that help prove that these deductions are allowed.

Special Situations

Records for the following need to be kept longer than any statute of limitations:

- ☐ Pension plan contributions and withdrawals (The IRS specifically requires individuals to keep copies of Forms 8606, 5498, and 1099-R as well as copies of your tax returns until all funds are withdrawn from your retirement accounts.)
- ☐ Expense records for excess losses that are carried forward and deducted in future years—such as records pertaining to passive activities, e.g., investments in limited partnerships;Expense records for tax write-offs that are calculated by the use of tax basis—such as:
  - Records of expenses associated with assets, property, or costs that are depreciated, amortized, or depleted over more than one year;
  - Expense records for business real estate and capital assets that will be subject to capital gains taxes on sale;
  - Brokerage statements and expense records that will be necessary to determine capital gains or losses upon the sale of investment securities.

Tax Returns

Keep copies of completed tax returns *forever*. These documents do not take up much space and are vital references for unforeseen future activities such as a merger or sale of the company.

Tax Filing

Amended Returns

As a general rule, a taxpayer has up to three years from the due date of a return to file an amended return. Unfortunately, these returns require special handling by the IRS. A process center employee has to pull the original return and then compare it with the amended filing. Each change and the magnitude of the difference from the original filing are reviewed. Those items that are questionable may be referred to an IRS examiner for a more thorough review. As a result, taxpayers are cautioned to weigh the benefits of filing an amended return against the significantly increased risk of audit. The decision to file an amended return is often greatly influenced by whether other items on the original filing can withstand the extra scrutiny of an auditor's review.

Nonpayment

> *"Some people as a result of adversity are sadder, wiser, kinder, more human. Most of us are better, though, when things go better."*
>
> —Malcolm Forbes

☑ Father Time is especially cruel to tax debtors—their financial burdens grow larger every day with mounting penalties and interest on the unpaid amounts. However, the penalties and interest will vary significantly (and may even be waived) depending upon the circumstances involved and the actions taken by the taxpayer.

One crucial thing to remember: If you are behind on taxes and want to stay in business, keep the IRS informed. Complete the necessary tax forms on time and send them in with as much of a partial payment as you can afford. By filing on time and thereby informing the IRS that there is a problem, the penalty and interest amounts will be much less.

Penalties and Interest

The delinquent taxpayer will be subject to a penalty of 0.5% to 1% of the unpaid tax for each month or part of a month that the tax is unpaid—up to a maximum of 25% of the tax due. He or she will also have to pay interest (at 3% over the short-term Treasury bill rate) on all unpaid amounts, which is compounded daily. It may be possible to avoid the penalty portion if the business owner can show that the failure to pay was due to a reasonable cause. Not having the money or not knowing about the tax are not reasonable causes. All business owners are expected to know the laws and to put aside enough money to cover their tax liabilities.

Failure to file a tax return will make the delinquent taxpayer subject to even steeper penalties. In fact, the penalty rises to 5% of the unpaid tax for each month (or part of a month) that the tax is unpaid—up to a maximum of 25% of the tax. The maximum 25% penalty will be assessed within five months (5 months times 5% per month). On the other hand, when a taxpayer files a return, the maximum 25% penalty is spread over 50 months (50 months times 0.5% penalty per month). In addition, a "failure to pay penalty" of at least $100 or the tax due, whichever is lower, may also apply when a return is more than 60 days late.

Filing an IRS Form 4868 prior to the due date of a tax filing will provide the taxpayer with an automatic six-month extension of the filing deadline. However, the filing of this form does not extend the payment deadline. All taxes must be paid by the original filing deadline. If they are not, the taxpayer will be assessed applicable interest and penalties.

IRS Challenges

In light of all this, the plus side is that the IRS collection machine is slow to start. It has limited resources and usually tries to avoid assigning a real person to a tax delinquency situation (except in the case of business payroll taxes). The minus side is that the IRS has legal powers that no other debt collector has. It can seize bank accounts or just about anything else the taxpayer owns—often without notice. Therefore, try to work with the IRS. Avoidance may give you time, but it will not make the tax liability go away. IRS Publication 594, *The IRS Collection Process*, will help. However, if the IRS does not accept an installment payment program (IRS Form 9465) or some other financially viable solution, you may need to discuss other alternatives with your legal and financial advisors, e.g., filing for personal bankruptcy protection.

☑ The IRS generally can come back and ask for more taxes within three years from the due date of the return. However, if a taxpayer neglects to report an item of income that amounts to 25% or more of his income, the IRS has up to six years to challenge the return. When fraud is suspected, the IRS can challenge a tax filing at any time. There are no statute of limitations on prosecuting and collecting the extra taxes that are due in the case of fraud.

CHAPTER

Deductions

"Anyone may so arrange his affairs that his taxes shall be low as possible; he is not bound to choose that pattern which will best pay the treasury; there is not even a patriotic duty to increase one's taxes."

—Learned Hand

The most generous tax shelter in America is to own a business—but only if you know what deductions are allowed, conduct your daily business to capture those deductions, and then properly file your tax return. Unfortunately, many business owners spend little time thinking about taxes until the tax year has ended. These naïve procrastinators assume that the trick to cutting taxes is to find the right accountant—someone who knows every footnote of the Tax Code and will uncover the perfect loophole that will magically slash their taxes. Tax season is the wrong time to look for magic or miracles. By then, there is little any tax professional can do other than to add up the columns. Maximizing the personal and wealth generating potential of your business requires tax planning and decisive tax-savvy actions throughout the year.

This chapter is the crux of tax-wise business ownership, i.e., business deductions. In fact, business deductions are the crucial component of all tax strategies. Intelligently utilized, they allow tax-wise business owners to significantly reduce and sometimes completely eliminate taxes—thereby offsetting some of the inherent financial risks of doing business.

The following expense deduction examples are some of the most important tax deductions that are available to business owners. Where there are differences in tax deductibility based on the business form (legal structure), included is an explanation of how the deduction is claimed for that particular type of business entity.

☑ Some business deductions are specifically identified in the Code; however, the vast majority are not. (See IRC §162.) What the IRS and the Code clearly allow (whether spelled out or not) are business tax deductions that are:

- ☐ Incurred in connection with a trade, business, or profession
- ☐ Ordinary, necessary, and reasonable

Accident and Health Benefits

Employers can generally deduct the cost of accident benefits and group health insurance plans for employees, former employees, and families of employees. The value of these benefits is generally excluded from the employee's wages.

The rules on deductibility of business-paid accident and health benefits are different for the owners than for their employees, unless the business is a C corporation.

S Corporation Shareholders

A 2% or greater shareholder of an S corporation who is also an employee is not eligible for the wage exclusion. The value of accident or health benefits provided to these shareholder employees must be included in their wages and are subject to federal income tax withholding. However, benefit values other than payments for specific injuries or illnesses are excluded from social security, Medicare, and federal unemployment (FUTA) taxes.

☑ *Example*
Joe Smith, the sole owner of an S corporation, ABC Plumbing, Inc. (ABC), purchases a group health plan for himself and his four employees. The $13,450 annual insurance premiums are 100% tax deductible to ABC. However, the portion attributable to Joe ($3,030) is taxable income to Joe. Fortunately, Joe can deduct the full amount on his individual income tax return as an adjustment to income.

If Joe's spouse, a non-owner, is one of the employees of ABC, Joe can fully deduct the cost of his health insurance as the spouse of an employee (IRC §105).

Affordable Care Act

The Patient Protection and Affordable Care Act (Affordable Care Act or ACA) enacted comprehensive health insurance reforms designed to provide Americans the opportunity to access to quality, affordable health insurance.

The ACA includes a variety of measures specifically for small businesses that help lower premium cost growth and increase access to quality, affordable health insurance. Based on whether you are self-employed, an employer with fewer than 25 employees, an employer with fewer than 50 employees, or an employer with 50 or more employees, different provisions of the ACA may be applicable to your business.

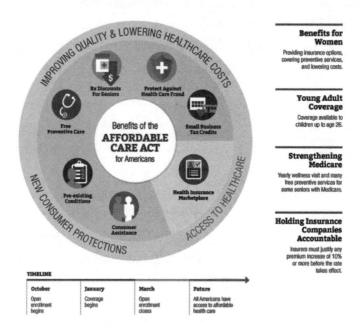

Self-Employed

Implementation of the ACA will occurred in steps, with many of the reforms and requirements taking effect in 2013 and 2014. Some of the provisions that impacted self-employed individuals included:

Individual Shared Responsibility Provisions. Starting in 2014, the Individual Shared Responsibility provisions of the ACA call for each individual to have basic health insurance coverage (known as minimum essential coverage), qualify for an exemption, or make a shared responsibility payment when filing a federal income tax return. Individuals do not have to make a payment if coverage is unaffordable, if they spend less than three consecutive months without coverage, or if they qualify for an exemption for several other reasons, including hardship and religious beliefs.

Minimum essential coverage includes, at a minimum, all of the following categories:

1. Employer-sponsored coverage (including COBRA and retiree coverage);
2. Coverage purchased in the individual market;
3. Medicare Part A coverage;
4. Medicaid coverage;
5. Children's Health Insurance Program (CHIP) coverage;
6. Certain types of Veterans health coverage; and
7. TRICARE.

Minimum essential coverage does not include certain specialized coverage such as only for vision or dental care, workers' compensation, or coverage only for a specific disease or condition.

Individual Insurance Marketplaces. The individual health insurance marketplaces offer a choice of four levels of benefit packages that differ by the percentage of costs the health plan covers. Individuals and the self-employed may qualify for individual tax credits and subsidies on a sliding scale, based on income.

Coverage through Medicaid Expansion. Each state operates a Medicaid program that provides health coverage for lower-income people, families and children, the elderly, and people with disabilities. The eligibility rules for Medicaid vary by state, but most states currently offer coverage for adults with children at some income level. In addition, under the ACA, states have the option to expand Medicaid eligibility to include adults ages 19—64 with incomes up to 133% of the Federal Poverty Level (about $15,000 per year for an individual, $31,000/year for a family of four).

New Medicare Assessment on Net Investment Income. Beginning in 2013, a 3.8% tax was assessed on net investment income such as taxable capital gains, dividends, rents, royalties, and interest for taxpayers with Modified Adjusted Gross Income (MAGI) over $200,000 for single filers and $250,000 for married joint filers. Common types of income that are not investment income are wages, unemployment compensation, operating income from a non-passive business, social security benefits, alimony, tax-exempt interest, and self-employment income.

Employers with Fewer Than 25 Employees

Small Business Health Care Tax Credits. The small business Health Care Tax Credit helps small employers afford the cost of health care coverage for their employees and was specifically targeted for those employers with low- and moderate-income workers. The credit is designed to encourage small employers to offer health insurance coverage for the first time or maintain coverage they already have. Since 2010, businesses that have fewer than 25 full-time equivalent employees (FTEs), pay average annual wages below $50,000, and that contribute 50% or more toward employees' self-only health insurance premiums may qualify for a small business tax credit of up to 35% to help offset the costs of insurance. In 2014, the tax credit increased to 50% and was available to qualified small employers that participate in the Small Business Health Options Program (SHOP). Eligible small employers were able to claim the current credit through 2013, and the enhanced credit can be claimed for any two consecutive taxable years beginning in 2014 through the SHOP.

Small Business Health Options Program (SHOP). Open for enrollment now, small employers with generally up to 50 employees will have access to the new health care insurance marketplaces through the Small Business Health Options Program (SHOP). Currently, small businesses may pay on average 18% more than big businesses for health insurance because of administrative costs. SHOP offers small employers increased purchasing power to obtain a better choice of high-quality coverage at a lower cost. Costs are lowered because small employers can pool their risk. To enroll, eligible employers must have an office within the service area of the SHOP and offer SHOP coverage to all full-time employees. In 2016, employers with up to 100 employees will be able to participate in SHOP.

Employer Notice to Employees of the New Health Insurance Marketplace. Under the ACA, employers covered by the Fair Labor Standards Act (generally, those firms that have at least one employee and at least $500,000 in annual dollar volume of business), must provide notification to their employees about the new Health Insurance Marketplace, inform employees that they may be eligible for a premium tax credit if they purchase coverage through the Marketplace, and advise employees that if they employee purchase a plan through the Marketplace, they may lose the employer contribution (if any) to any health benefits plan offered by the employer.

Summary of Benefits and Coverage (SBCs) Disclosure Rules. Employers are required to provide employees with a standard "Summary of Benefits and Coverage" form explaining what their plan covers and what it costs. The purpose of the SBC form is to help employees better understand and evaluate their health insurance options. Penalties may be imposed for non-compliance.

Medical Loss Ratio Rebates. Under the ACA, insurance companies must spend at least 80% of premium dollars on medical care rather than administrative costs. Insurers who do not meet this ratio are required to provide rebates to their policyholders, which is typically an employer who provides a group health plan. Employers who receive these premium rebates must determine whether the rebates constitute plan assets. If treated as a plan asset, employers have discretion to determine a reasonable and fair allocation of the rebate.

Limits on Flexible Spending Account Contributions. For plan years beginning on or after January 2013, the maximum amount an employee may elect to contribute to health care flexible spending arrangements (FSAs) for any year is capped at $2,500, subject to cost-of-living adjustments. Note that the limit only applies to elective employee contributions and does not extend to employer contributions.

Additional Medicare Withholding on Wages. Beginning in 2013, ACA increased the employee portion of the Medicare Part A Hospital Insurance (HI) withholdings by .9% (from 1.45% to 2.35%) on employees with incomes of over $200,000 for single filers and $250,000 for married joint filers. It is the employer's obligation to withhold this additional tax, which applies only to wages in excess of these thresholds. The employer portion of the tax is unchanged at 1.45%.

New Medicare Assessment on Net Investment Income. Beginning in 2013, a 3.8% tax was assessed on net investment income such as taxable capital gains, dividends, rents, royalties, and interest for taxpayers with Modified Adjusted Gross Income (MAGI) over $200,000 for single filers and $250,000 for married couples filing jointly.

90-Day Maximum Waiting Period. Beginning January 1, 2014, individuals who are eligible for employer-provided health coverage are not required to wait more than 90 days to begin coverage.

Transitional Reinsurance Program Fees. The Transitional Reinsurance Program, a three-year program which began in 2014 and continues until 2016, and reimburses insurers in the individual insurance Marketplaces for high claims costs. The program is funded through fees to be paid by employers (for self-insured plans) and insurers (for insured plans). The fee applies to all employer-sponsored plans providing major medical coverage, including retiree programs. The U.S. Department of Labor has advised that for self-insured plans, these fees can be paid from plan assets, and the IRS stated that the fees are tax deductible for employers.

Workplace Wellness Programs. The ACA created new incentives to promote employer wellness programs and encourage employers to take more opportunities to support healthier workplaces. Health-contingent wellness programs generally require individuals to meet a specific standard related to their health to obtain a reward, such as programs that provide a reward to employees who don't use, or decrease their use of, tobacco, and programs that reward employees who achieve a specified level of lower cholesterol. Under final rules that were effective January 1, 2014, the maximum reward to employers using a health-contingent wellness program will increase from 20 percent to 30 percent of the cost of health coverage. Additionally, the maximum reward for programs designed to prevent or reduce tobacco use will be as much as 50 percent. The final rules also allow for flexibility in the types of wellness programs employers can offer.

Health Insurance Coverage Reporting Requirements. Beginning in 2015, the ACA provides for new information reporting by employers that sponsor self-insured plans. Self-funded employers, issuers, and other parties that provide health coverage must submit these new reports to the IRS detailing information for each covered individual. The first of these reports must be filed in 2016.

Employers with Up to 50 Employees

This group has key provisions as were described above:

- ☐ Small Business Health Options Program (SHOP)
- ☐ Employer Notice to Employees of the New Health Insurance Marketplace
- ☐ Summary of Benefits and Coverage (SBCs) Disclosure Rules
- ☐ Medical Loss Ratio Rebates
- ☐ Limits on Flexible Spending Account Contributions
- ☐ Additional Medicare Withholding on Wages
- ☐ New Medicare Assessment on Net Investment Income
- ☐ 90-Day Maximum Waiting Period

- ☐ Transitional Reinsurance Program Fees
- ☐ Workplace Wellness Programs
- ☐ Health Insurance Coverage Reporting Requirements

Employers with 50 or More Employees

This group has key provisions as were described above, as well as others described below:

- ☐ Employer Notice to Employees of the New Health Insurance Marketplace
- ☐ Health Insurance Coverage Reporting Requirements
- ☐ Summary of Benefits and Coverage (SBCs) Disclosure Rules
- ☐ Medical Loss Ratio Rebates
- ☐ Limits on Flexible Spending Account Contributions
- ☐ Additional Medicare Withholding on Wages
- ☐ New Medicare Assessment on Net Investment Income
- ☐ 90-Day Maximum Waiting Period
- ☐ Transitional Reinsurance Program Fees
- ☐ Workplace Wellness Programs

W-2 Reporting of Aggregate Health Care Costs. Beginning January 2013, most employers were required to report the aggregate annual cost of employer-provided coverage for each employee on the Form W-2. The new W-2 reporting requirement is informational only and it does not require taxation on any health plan coverage. Reporting is required for most employer-sponsored health coverage, including group medical coverage. Small Employer Exception: For 2012 reporting and beyond until further guidance is issued, the W-2 reporting requirement does not apply to employers required to file fewer than 250 Form W-2s in the prior calendar year.

Employer Shared Responsibility Provisions. Beginning in 2015, employers with 50 or more full-time/full-time equivalent employees that do not offer affordable health insurance that provides minimum value to their full-time employees (and dependents) may be required to pay an assessment if at least one of their full-time employees is certified to receive a premium tax credit in an individual health insurance Marketplace. The assessment, known as Employer Shared Responsibility, will offset part of the cost of the Marketplace premium tax credits. Treasury issued transitional relief to employers covered by these rules indicating that no shared responsibility payments would apply until 2015.

Accounting and Bookkeeping

Most owners think of an accountant or a bookkeeper as an employee hired to keep track of the financial transactions of their business. The salary paid to these types of employees is a current expense, but it is not the subject of this deduction. Here we are talking about fees paid to third parties, which cover a wide range of different services, i.e., accounting, bookkeeping, payroll calculating, tax return preparation, auditing, tax advice, etc.

Accounting and bookkeeping fees are deductible, as are business consultations with your CPA. However, these expenses cover a much wider range than simply filling out tax returns or tracking what money comes in and out of your business. Such services may include oversight and compliance with withholding laws and other special tax laws that apply to your type of business.

Example

Joe Smith owns and operates a small mini-mart. He hires an independent financial consultant to maintain the books for his business as well as his personal finances. The consultant charges Joe a monthly fee of $300 for both services. At tax time, Joe may not deduct the full amount of these charges. He may only deduct the proportional amount of fees that directly pertained to his business at the mini-mart. Joe determines that two-thirds of the fee was for business and one-third was personal. Therefore, Joe can claim a business deduction of $200 a month ($300 minus $100) for mini-mart bookkeeping expenses.

☑ *Caution*: Owners who are sole proprietors can only deduct the bookkeeping expenses that are actually associated with their businesses. This is a cautionary note, because there is often a fine line between a sole proprietor's personal and business activities. For example, only the preparation of the business part of the sole proprietor's 1040 tax return (schedule C and related schedules) is a deductible business expense.

Note: The deductibility of accounting and other professional fees incurred in preparation for starting a business as well as expenses associated with buying a business come under special rules. (See these sections in this chapter: Amortizable Costs and Business Set-Up Expenses.)

Achievement Awards

A business can generally deduct (within specified limits) amounts paid to employees as achievement awards, whether paid in cash or property. (For awards paid in property, see Property.) An achievement award is an item of tangible personal property or cash that is given to an employee for a length of service or safety achievement. An award must be part of a meaningful presentation and cannot be awarded under conditions or circumstances that create a significant likelihood that it is disguised pay.

Awards that are qualified plan awards (i.e., given as part of an established written plan or program that does not favor highly compensated employees) are deductible up to a limit of $1,600 per employee during a tax year. All other awards are deductible up to a limit of $400 per employee during a tax year. (For additional restrictions, refer to IRS Publications 535, *Business Expenses* and 15-B, *Employer's Tax Guide to Fringe Benefits*.)

Adoption Assistance

Employers may deduct the payments or reimbursements (up to $13,460 per qualifying child in 2016) that are made to employees under qualified adoption assistance programs or for the adoption of children with special needs. The employee does not have to include the adoption assistance in wages. (See Fringe Benefits.)

☑ *S Corporation Shareholders*
A 2% or greater shareholder of an S corporation who is also an employee is not eligible for the wage exclusion. The value of the adoption assistance provided to these shareholder employees must be included in their wages and are subject to federal income tax withholding and social security, Medicare, and federal unemployment (FUTA) taxes.

Advertising

See Promotion (Advertising).

Appraisals

Appraisal fees paid to determine the value of assets and properties as well as those that are conducted to establish the amount of a loss are generally deductible. Obviously, certain business assets that are used to secure loans or that are subject to taxes based on value, such as real estate, may need to be appraised from time to time. Appraisal fees for real estate are 100% deductible. (See Real Estate.)

Often, appraisals of business ownership interests, such as partnership or LLC interests and equity in corporations, are completed prior to a transfer of ownership. If this appraisal is conducted by a C corporation in order to value its stock, the fees are 100% deductible. However, if the appraisal is done for the sale or purchase of a business, the expense will probably have to be capitalized. In this case, the appraisal fee is still deductible, but the tax deduction is spread over a period of months (amortized) rather than deducted as a current expense in the year it was incurred. (See these sections in this chapter: Amortizable Costs and Business Set-Up Expenses.)

Example

Joe Smith founded Joe's Plumbing and Curios, Inc. as a C corporation many years ago. Joe still owns all of the stock in the company but decides he would like to sell off the curio division of his company. In order to sell the division, Joe completes a full business appraisal to establish the value of his stock and the portion that is attributable to this division. The cost was $5,000 and it was 100% deductible to Joe's C corporation. If Joe had formed his company in any other legal form, i.e. sole proprietorship, partnership, LLC, or S corporation, the appraisal fees would probably have to be amortized.

Assessments

Often, the need arises to make local municipal improvements that will benefit property owners within a limited area, i.e., paving streets, installing curbs, sewers, etc. Such improvements are typically provided through special assessments on property. The area receiving the improvements is the improvement district or assessment district. Costs are apportioned to owners according to the benefits received, rather than by the value of the land and buildings being assessed. For example, in a commercial area, the assessment for installation of storm drains, curbs, and gutters is usually made on a front-foot basis.

A property owner is charged for each foot of his lot that abuts the street being improved.

☑ The underlying theory of special assessments is that the improvements must benefit the land against which the cost will be charged, and the value of the benefits must exceed the cost. Although this is the theory, local governments often pay for repairing sidewalks, streets, sewers, etc. through special assessments. These assessments are generally tax-deductible as a current expense provided that the money is used to maintain rather than increase the value of the real estate. However, when the assessment is for new construction that actually increases the value of the property, the assessment is not deductible. Rather, the assessment is depreciable over 15 years under the general depreciation system (GDS) or amortizable over 20 years under the alternate depreciation system (ADS). (See IRS Publication 946, *How To Depreciate Property*, Table B-1, Asset class 00.3 Land Improvements.)

Example

Joe Smith owns and operates a small mini-mart in the town of Black Acre. The municipal government decides that it is going to repair the water lines in town and add sidewalks. To pay for the repairs of the water lines and construct the new sidewalks, Joe's property is assessed $7,500 for the water line repair and $8,250 for new sidewalks.

Joe can take a current tax deduction for 100% of the assessment that is for the water line repair ($7,500). However, Joe must depreciate the assessment that is for the construction of the sidewalks ($8,250).

Associations—Clubs

Congress has banned business deductions for membership dues paid to country clubs and many other types of business, athletic, and social organizations. Although the ban seems to apply broadly, the IRS lists several types of membership organizations for which the dues are still generally 100% deductible. These include:

- ☐ Professional associations, i.e., bar and medical associations
- ☐ Public service organizations, i.e., Rotary, Lions etc.
- ☐ Business trade groups, i.e., chambers of commerce

However, dues or membership fees in athletic clubs or other recreational or pleasure clubs are not tax deductible. (See Athletic Facilities.)

Example

Joe Smith owns a computer software company. Joe pays membership dues of $500 a year to the Chamber of Commerce. Joe may deduct the dues as a business expense.

Athletic Facilities

The fees and dues for memberships in athletic clubs are not a deductible business expense. However, businesses may deduct the cost of operating an on-premises (owned or leased) gym or other athletic facilities that are used only by employees, their spouses, and their dependent children. The value of the benefit is excluded from the wages of employees.

Note: This deduction and wage exclusion does not apply to athletic facilities for residential or resort use.

If the athletic facility is built by the business, the construction costs can be recovered as a depreciation or amortization expense over the life of the facility. The athletic equipment may be deducted as a Section 179 expense or depreciated or amortized using Form 4562, *Depreciation and Amortization*.

Example

Joe Smith owns an S corporation with 800 employees. His business operations are confined to a single commercial site that Joe also owns. He believes that employee productivity will increase if they can relieve stress by working out in a gym during the day.

If Joe decides to pay membership fees for his employees to use a local gym, the fees will not be deductible as a business expense. In addition, each employee will have to pay income tax on the value of his or her membership. Alternatively, if Joe builds a gym on the business premises, the cost of operating the gym is 100% deductible and the use of the facility is a nontaxable fringe benefit for his employees.

Attorney Fees

My personal favorite—fees paid to business lawyers are 100% deductible. Also included in this category are accounting fees, tax preparation fees, auditing services, and other similar services.

Example

Joe Smith owns and operates a small mini-mart where a customer slips and falls. The customer sues Joe. Joe retains his lawyer for the lawsuit and fortunately succeeds at trial.

Joe filed a counter claim to recover the cost of the attorney's fees. He regrettably was not awarded such fees, but fortunately for Joe, he can deduct 100% of the attorney's fees as a necessary business deduction.

Autos

See Vehicles.

Bad Debts

"Credit is like a looking glass, which, when once sullied by a breath, may be wiped clear again, but if once cracked can never be repaired."

—Sir Walter Scott

A business bad debt is a loss from the worthlessness of a debt that was either:

- ☐ Created or acquired in your trade of business or
- ☐ Closely related to your trade or business when it became partly or totally worthless

Note: The bad debts of a corporation are always business bad debts.

Regardless of their source, a business can take a bad debt deduction only if the amount owed was previously included in gross income. This rule applies to amounts owed to the business from all sources of taxable income, including sales, services, rents, and interest (IRS Publication 535, *Business Expenses*, Chapter 10, Business Bad Debts, IRC §162 and §166). For example, a sole proprietor cannot take a bad debt deduction for services performed for a client who does not pay because the income has not been posted on the sole proprietor's financial ledger. Therefore, in this situation, the bad debt deduction would have no offsetting income and would not be allowed. The sole proprietor does not get an additional deduction for the income that he should have earned. However, out-of-pocket expenses incurred by the taxpayer are deductible as current expenses.

In addition to the income inclusion requirement cited above, for a bad debt to qualify for a deduction:

☐ The debt must be bona fide
☐ There must be evidence of total or partial worthlessness

A debt is a bona fide debt when a true creditor/debtor relationship exists. This means that:

☐ There is a legal obligation to repay the debt
☐ Money loaned came from the party or business claiming the bad debt deduction

The next requirement to establish a bad debt (evidence of worthlessness) is more ambiguous. A debtor's notice of nonpayment does not, in itself, prove that the debt is worthless. A debt becomes worthless when there is no longer any chance that the amount owed will be paid. It is up to the claimant to show that the terms of the note were enforced and that adequate and reasonable steps to collect were attempted. It is not necessary to go to court if the claimant can show that a judgment from the court would be uncollectible. Documenting the bankruptcy or insolvency of the debtor most often evidence this.

Business bad debts are mainly the result of unpaid credit sales to customers, i.e., goods and services recorded as accounts or notes receivable. However, there are many other situations that may result in business bad debts:

- ☐ Loans made for business reasons to clients, suppliers, employees, or distributors that become worthless;
- ☐ Business debts of an insolvent partner that are paid by the remaining partners of a partnership;
- ☐ Business loan guarantees that are exercised to pay a debt;
- ☐ The sale of mortgaged property for less that the outstanding balance of the mortgage.

☑ *Note*: If two or more debtors jointly owe money, the inability to collect from one party does not allow the others to deduct a proportionate amount as a bad debt.

Business bad debts are deductible. However, the deduction is limited to the uncollected balance of the indebtedness.

Example

Joe Smith owns and operates a computer software company. Joe sells software directly to computer manufactures to be installed on new machines. A customer, ABC, Inc. (ABC), filed for bankruptcy. At the time of the bankruptcy filing, ABC owed Joe's company $30,000. The trustee in receivership for the bankruptcy of ABC paid the creditors $0.05 on the dollar. Joe's company received $1,500 ($30,000 times .05 = $1,500) as final payment on the ABC account.

Joe's company may deduct the remaining unpaid balance of the ABC account, i.e., $28,500 as a bad debt deduction ($30,000 minus the $1,500 paid by the trustee).

Bank Fees

The costs of maintaining a checking, savings, or other banking account is fully deductible to a business. This includes service charges, penalties, check printing costs, and fees associated with lines of credit, credit cards, and other banking-related transactions.

Example

Joe Smith owns and operates a small mini-mart. He opens a checking account for the mini-mart with AB Bank. At the end of the tax year, Joe's accountant reviews the mini-mart bank statements. He finds that Joe paid $30 in penalties for not maintaining the required minimum account balance, $60 in service fees for processing returned checks, and a $15 fee for printing the checks for the account. Joe will be able to deduct a total of $105 for all fees associated with the bank account as an ordinary business expense.

Bartering

Bartering is the exchange of your goods or services for someone else's business goods or services. Business owners often overlook bartering income and expenses when they calculate their taxes, but these exchanges are taxable and must be reported.

☑ A business subtracts the fair market value (FMV) of its goods or services from the FMV of those received to calculate the income or loss from a bartered transaction. On the surface, this is a straightforward mathematical calculation. In fact, because it is dependent on the determination of FMVs, bartering creates an area that is ripe for abuse. The IRS knows this and it has a tendency to expand audits when bartering is involved. Tax-wise business owners will protect themselves by obtaining credible third-party appraisals of bartering FMVs whenever possible.

Example

Joe Smith owns a small plumbing business and Mike Doe owns a small roofing business. Joe and Mike decide to barter for each other's services. Under the terms of their agreement

- Joe will provide services with a FMV of $9,500 to plumb Mike's new business building;
- Mike will provide services with a FMV of $7,500 to re-roof Joe's business building.

Since most of the value of the plumbing is for his personal labor, Joe has decided that the "opportunity costs" outweigh the difference in relative FMVs, i.e., $2,000 ($9,500 minus $7,500).

Joe may deduct the FMV of $9,500 for his services, provided that he claims income of $7,500 for the FMV of the services performed by Mike. Joe is able to claim a net loss of $2,000 from the bartered transaction. Mike may deduct the $7,500 FMV of his services, but must claim income of $9,500 for the FMV of the service provided by Joe. Mike has a net gain of $2,000 from the bartered transaction.

The IRS audits both Joe and Mike the following year. It finds that Mike's services were valued correctly, but the true FMV of Joe's services was $7,500. Joe owes the IRS for back taxes plus penalties and interest for not paying on time because his FMV error caused him to claim a $2,000 deduction on his tax return.

Bonuses

Businesses can deduct a bonus paid to an employee if:

- ☐ Intended as additional pay for services (not as a gift);
- ☐ For services that were actually performed by the employee;
- ☐ The total of bonuses, salaries, and other pay is reasonable for the services provided by the employee.

The IRC classifies bonuses and other incentives paid to employees as wages. These payments are deductible to the employer and are considered compensation to employees and therefore subject to payroll taxes and withholding laws.

Example

Joe Smith owns a small mini-mart where Mike Doe is an employee. Because Mike is such a great employee and has a great work ethic, Joe decided to give Mike a $2,000 bonus. Joe may claim the $2,000 as a payroll deduction, and Mike must claim the $2,000 as employment compensation for tax purposes.

Business Set Up Expenses

When a business is first set up, all expenses incurred before the business is ready to take work from, or provide services to, customers are considered capital expenses. These costs have to be either included in the basis (the starting value of the business and its assets) or amortized. Business owners who choose to amortize certain costs must do so over a period of at least 60 months (IRC §195). However, in order to be an allowable amortizable deduction for setting up a business, an expense must qualify as one of the following:

- ☐ A business startup cost
- ☐ An organizational cost for a corporation
- ☐ An organizational cost for a partnership

Startup Costs

Startup costs are costs for creating an active trade or business or investigating the creation or acquisition of an active trade or business. This includes any amounts paid or incurred in connection with any activity engaged in for profit and for the production of income in anticipation that the activity will become an active trade or business.

A startup cost is amortizable if it meets both of the following tests:

1. It is a cost the taxpayer could deduct if it were paid or incurred to operate an existing active business in the same field.
2. It is a cost paid or incurred before the day the business actively begins.

Startup costs include:

- ☐ Analyses and surveys of markets, products, competitors, labor force, location, transportation, etc.
- ☐ Pre-opening advertising and market expenses
- ☐ Salaries and wages of employees in training and their instructors
- ☐ Travel and other necessary costs to secure prospective distributors, suppliers, or customers
- ☐ Salaries and fees for executives and consultants or for similar professional services

The key determinant for startup expenses is the date that the business actively begins. This might be when the business is ready to accept customers; however, the actual event that triggers being in business (as opposed to starting a business) will vary according to the type of business and the way that it is operated. From a taxation standpoint, a tax-wise business owner may want to postpone as many business purchases as possible until after the business has started. These postponed expenses would probably be more tax-advantaged to the owner as deductible expenses and/or depreciable assets—rather than startup costs that must be amortized over at least a 180-month period.

Startup costs that do not qualify for amortization include deductible interest, taxes, or research and experimental costs.

Corporation Organizational Costs

A direct cost associated with the creation of a corporation can be amortized if it meets all of the following tests:

1. It is for the creation of the corporation.
2. It is chargeable to a capital account, i.e., it adds to the basis in the business.
3. It could be amortized over the life of the corporation if the corporation had a fixed life.
4. It is incurred before the end of the first tax year in which the corporation is in business.

The following are examples of organizational costs:

☐ The cost of temporary directors
☐ The cost of organizational meetings
☐ State incorporation fees

- ☐ The cost of accounting services for setting up the corporation
- ☐ The cost of legal services (such as drafting of the charter, bylaws, terms of the original stock certificates, and minutes of organizational meetings)

The following costs are examples of capital expenditures associated with forming a corporation that cannot be amortized:

- ☐ Costs for issuing and selling stock or securities such as commissions, professional fees, and printing costs
- ☐ Costs associated with the transfer of assets to the corporation such as real estate transfer fees

Partnership Organizational Costs

A direct cost incurred for the organization of a partnership can be amortized if it meets all of the following tests:

1. It is for creating rather than operating the partnership.
2. It is chargeable to a capital account, i.e., it adds to the basis of the partnership.
3. It could be amortized over the life of the partnership if the partnership had a fixed life.
4. It is incurred prior to the due date of the partnership's first tax return (including extensions).
5. It is for an item that is expected to be of benefit throughout the life of the partnership.

Partnership organizational costs that can be amortized include the following fees:

- ☐ Legal fees for services such as negotiating and preparing the partnership agreement
- ☐ Accounting fees for setting up financial controls for the partnership
- ☐ Filing fees, such as work permits

The following costs cannot be amortized:

- ☐ The cost of acquiring assets or transferring assets to the partnership;
- ☐ The cost of admitting or removing partners other than at the time of initial partnership organization;
- ☐ The cost of making a contract for the operation of the partnership's trade or business (including contracts between partners and the partnership);
- ☐ The cost of issuing and marketing interests in the partnership (such as brokerage, registration, and legal fees; and printing costs). These "syndication fees" are capital expenses that cannot be depreciated or amortized.

Example

Joe Smith decides that he would like to own and operate a plumbing business. He goes to tech school to learn the profession so that he can qualify for a trade degree. After spending two years of his life in the school, Joe hires a law firm to assist him in selecting a business structure and preparing documents for a municipal business license. At the same time, he starts to attend a series of seminars about starting a service business in preparation for opening his new firm, JS Plumbing.

The tech school classes cost Joe $10,000, and the business organizational fees and seminar expenses cost an additional $6,000. The technical training that Joe received would not be considered a startup expense since the business was not formed when the education took place. However, the other $6,000 are considered startup and organizational expenses, and Joe will be able amortize these costs over 60 months ($1,200 per year).

☑ If a business is organized as a corporation or a partnership, the corporation or the partnership is the only entity that can choose to amortize allowable set up expenses (IRC §248 and §709). The business owners, as shareholders or partners, cannot make this choice. This means that an individual shareholder or partner cannot amortize any costs incurred in setting up a corporation or partnership—only the corporation or partnership itself can elect to amortize these costs.

Charitable Contributions

☑ Charitable contributions are a particularly sticky area in the Tax Code. In this area, the legal structure of the business makes a significant difference in how charitable contributions are deducted. In fact, only C corporations can take a business deduction for a charitable contribution. All other business forms pass charitable contribution deductions through to their respective owners. Each owner (members of

LLCs or partners of partnerships) claims his pro rata share of the charitable contributions when he files his personal Form 1040 tax return.

To claim a charitable contribution, the receiving entity must be an IRS approved charity. In the case of C corporations, there is some confusion as to whether a well-publicized donation is a charitable contribution or actually an advertising expense. In either case, the C corporation should receive the deduction.

Example

Joe Smith owns and operates a small plumbing business as a sole proprietor. Joe gives a $250 charitable donation to the Red Cross in the name of his plumbing business. Joe may not take the deduction as a business deduction. He must claim the contribution on his personal Form 1040 as a charitable donation.

Cleaning Services

Janitorial and other cleaning services for a business are deductible. This includes the cleaning of all business buildings and facilities as well as certain laundry services, such as:

- ☐ Cleaning costs for employee uniforms and required personal protective gear
- ☐ The cost of laundry services during overnight business trips

Example

Joe Smith owns and operates a computer software company. Joe hires a janitorial service for $2,000 a month to clean his business offices. The monthly fee covers man-hour costs ($1,700), supplies ($100), and uniform cleaning costs ($200). Joe may deduct the entire $2,000 as a janitorial business expense.

Communications —Telephone and Cell Phone Fees

The cost of telephone, cellular, and pager services are generally 100% deductible. The exception is for business owners who qualify for a home office deduction. In this case, no deduction is allowed for any portion of the basic line charge for the first phone line coming into the taxpayer's home.

Computer Software

Typically, the cost of computer software that is readily available for purchase by the general public may be depreciated over three years using a straight-line depreciation method. There are two exceptions to this three-year rule:

1. If the useful life of the computer software is less than three years, the cost may be depreciated over its useful life. For example, a tax preparation program that is only good for the year in which it is purchased is 100% depreciable in that year.
2. The other exception to the three-year rule is software that was bundled with a computer when purchased. In this case, the bundled software is considered part of the computer, and computers are depreciable over five years. (See Information Systems — Computers and Peripherals.)

As always, the business may opt to claim the entire cost of computer software in the year purchased as a Section 179 deduction. (See Section 179 Deductions in Chapter 4 and IRS Publication 946, Chapter 2, *Electing the Section 179 Deduction*.)

Computers and Peripherals

See Information Systems—Computers and Peripherals.

Conventions

Business owners and employers can deduct travel expenses and other business expenses for attending a convention or seminar in North America if they can show that attendance benefits their trade or business. However, if the convention or seminar is for investment, political, social, or other purposes unrelated to the trade or business, the expenses cannot be deducted regardless of the location. (For convention expense deductions and a definition of North American area, refer to IRS Publication 463, Chapter 1, *Travel*.)

Expenses for attending a convention, seminar, or similar meeting outside North America are not deductible unless both of the following are met:

1. The meeting is directly related to the owner's or employer's trade or business;
2. There is a reasonable explanation why the meeting was outside North American.

If the convention or seminar is held on a cruise ship—numerous additional rules apply, involving

- ☐ The ship's country of registration must be the U.S.;
- ☐ All of the cruise ship's ports of call must be in the U.S. or in possessions of the United States;
- ☐ Documentation of time spent on business activities is required;
- ☐ Written and signed attendance reports are required.

If all the rules are met, a business owner or employer may deduct expenses up to $2,000 per year per individual attending conventions, seminars, or similar meetings held on cruise ships. (All ships that sail are considered cruise ships.)

☑ If you plan to attend conventions overseas or on a cruise ship, be sure you understand all the rules governing deductibility of your trip before you make the arrangements. Otherwise, expense deductions could be denied. (See IRS Publication 463, *Travel, Entertainment, Gift, and Car Expenses*, and these sections in this chapter: Education, Entertainment, Meals, Seminars, and Travel.)

Credit Cards

"A credit card is a money tool, not a supplement to money. The failure to make this distinction has supplemented many a poor soul right into bankruptcy."

—Paula Nelson

All the costs and fees associated with the business use of a credit card are deductible. It is advisable to keep business and personal credit card accounts completely separate. Sole proprietors who use a personal credit card for both business and personal expenses may only deduct the prorated portion of these fees that are attributable to business. Other credit card expenses such as merchant fees and the costs associated with processing credit cards on behalf of clients are also 100% deductible.

☑ *Caution*: Review merchant account documents carefully before entering into an agreement. It is particularly important to avoid agreements that do not allow the business to keep the interest earned on monies held in suspense accounts. This will be important when the credit card company holds back payments pending the resolution of disputes, etc.

De Minimis (Minimal) Benefits

A de minimis benefit is any property or service that is provided by an employer to an employee that has so little value—taking into account how frequently similar benefits are provided to all employees—that accounting for it would be unreasonable or administratively impracticable. A de minimis benefit is 100% tax deductible by the employer, and its value is not reported as income to the receiving employee. (See IRS Publications 15-B, *Employer's Tax Guide to Fringe Benefits*, and 535, *Business Expenses*.)

Note: Cash, no matter how little, is never a de minimis benefit, except for occasional meal money or transportation fare.

Examples of de minimis benefits include the following:

☐ Occasional personal use of a company copying machine

- ☐ Holiday gifts, other than cash, with a low FMV
- ☐ Group-term life insurance on an employee's spouse or dependent if the face amount is not more than $2,000
- ☐ De minimis meals (See Meals)
- ☐ Occasional parties or picnics for employees and their guests
- ☐ Occasional tickets for entertainment or sporting events
- ☐ De minimis transportation fare for commuting

Dependent Care Assistance

A business may deduct dependent care assistance given to its employees either directly, by providing these services, or indirectly, through a set payment or reimbursement policy. The assistance must be for the care of an employee's qualified dependents and it must allow the employee to work. Under these circumstances, the employer can generally exclude $5,000 of benefits from an employee's wages ($2,500 for married employees filing separate returns).

Note: In general, employers may not exclude dependent care assistance from the wages of highly compensated employees. For 2013, highly compensated employees are those who meet either of the following tests:

1. The employee was a 5% or more owner of the business at any time during the tax year or the preceding year.

2. The employee received more than $115,000 in pay for the preceding year. This test can be ignored if the employee was not in the top 20% of employees when ranked by pay for the preceding year.

Example

Joe Smith owns a computer software company, XYZ Solutions, Inc. This C corporation provides a childcare service to employees at its headquarters building. XYZ may deduct the expense of operating the childcare service. Most employees need not include the value of such services on their Form 1040 tax filings.

Deposits

Deposits fall into two categories—refundable and nonrefundable.

For nonrefundable retainers or deposits, the Code allows a tax deduction when the nonrefundable funds are paid—provided that the underlying expense that the funds pay for is tax deductible.

Refundable deposits cannot be deducted unless:

☐ The deposits pay for expenses that are tax deductible

☐ The event that triggers a reduction in the deposit has occurred

Example

When a taxpayer prepays rent, the prepaid deposit is not deductible until the period in which the rent would normally have been due.

There are very narrow exceptions to these rules. Therefore, business owners should discuss the tax ramifications of prepayment deposits with their legal and tax advisors prior to making large deposits. An accountant will generally be able to determine when the deposit will be tax deductible—either on the date that the deposit is made or when the expense is actually incurred.

Example

Joe Smith owns and operates a small plumbing business. He rents a backhoe for a plumbing job and pays a $25 deposit that is refundable if the backhoe is returned by December 31, 2013. Joe also pays an additional $10 nonrefundable deposit on the same backhoe to cover the normal wear and tear of operation. The plumbing project takes longer than Joe expects and he does not return returns the backhoe until January 1, 2014.

Joe may deduct the $10 nonrefundable deposit in 2013. Joe may also deduct the $25 refundable deposit because he returned the backhoe late and forfeited his deposit. However, the deduction for the late return must be made on Joe's 2014 business tax filing because January 1, 2014, was the triggering date for this expense.

Directors' Fees

By default, directors of organizations are not considered employees. Payments to directors for their services are not subject to payroll taxes. However, all directors must pay self-employment taxes on the compensation. (See Taxes, the Self-Employment Tax.)

The IRC's definition of compensation is very broad. It includes monetary payments as well as fringe benefits that may be partially or completely tax-free. Whatever form compensation to directors may take, the amount paid and the costs of the fringe benefits given are 100% deductible to the organization making them.

Example

Joe Smith owns 100% of the stock of a computer software corporation, ABC Soft, Inc. (ABC). Joe is the chairman of the board of directors of ABC, but he is not an employee. Joe is paid $40,000 a year for his services as a director. ABC does not withhold payroll taxes but does provide Joe with a Form 1099 that shows the $40,000 he was paid. ABC may deduct the $40,000 as a business expense. Joe must pay self-employment tax on the $40,000 compensation he received as a director of ABC.

Discounts

An employer can generally exclude from wages the value of an employee discount that is provided to current, retired, and disabled former employees—as well as partners who perform services for a partnership.

The excluded discount is limited to

- 20% of the price charged to nonemployee customers for services
- The gross profit percentage times the price charged nonemployee customers for merchandise or other property

Dividends—Corporate Distributions

Dividends are distributions of money, stock, or other property paid to a shareholder by a C corporation. Dividends may also be made by any business entity that has elected to be taxed as a C corporation, i.e., a partnership, an estate, a trust, an association, or an LLC. Dividends, unlike wages, are not tax deductible to the corporation.

Most dividends are paid in cash (check); however, they can consist of more stock, stock rights, other property, or services. (See IRS Publication 550, *Investment Income and Expenses*.) The most common kinds of distributions are:

- Ordinary dividends
- Capital gain dividends
- Nontaxable dividends

Note: Some amounts that are called dividends are actually interest income.

Ordinary Dividends

Ordinary (taxable) dividends are the most common type of distribution from a C corporation. They are paid out of the earnings and profits of a corporation and are not tax deductible. Ordinary dividends are taxed as ordinary income to the shareholders.

If the shareholder is a natural person, the individual must pay taxes on ordinary dividends at his or her ordinary rate. This means that the money received as an ordinary dividend is taxed twice. Some accountants and business owners are adverse to the C corporation's business structure because of the double taxation on shareholders' dividends (distributions).

☑ Most small, closely held, C corporations are reluctant to declare and pay ordinary dividends. These firms generally hire key shareholders as executive employees. This allows the C corporation to deduct 100% of the wages and other compensation paid to these employee / shareholders. If compensation is found to be unreasonable by the IRS, then amounts paid to owners under the label of compensation will be treated as disguised dividends. *Result:* The company loses its tax deduction for the payment, but the owners must still report the income.

However, there are segments of the financial and legal services industries that are dedicated to helping C corporations shelter profits and make distributions to shareholders as tax efficiently as possible. For example, a tax break reserved for C corporations is the "dividends received" exclusion. This provision in the Code allows a C corporation to receive dividends 70% tax-free from stock it owns in another unrelated corporation. This is a highly technical area that is best handled by a tax professional.

Example

Joe Smith is the founder of a computer software corporation, ABC Soft, Inc. (ABC), a C corporation. Joe is a 51% stockholder of ABC. The board of directors of ABC decides to pay shareholders an ordinary dividend of $10,000 this year. Joe must include the $5,100 ordinary dividend (51% of $10,000) as income on his Form 1040 filing. ABC cannot deduct the $10,000 dividend that it paid to its stockholders.

Capital Gain Dividends

Capital gain dividends are paid to shareholders by regulated investment companies (mutual funds) and real estate investment trusts (REITs). These highly specialized businesses are subject to numerous regulations that are beyond the scope of this book. Capital gain dividends are reported by shareholders as long-term capital gains, regardless of how long the shares in the mutual fund or REIT have been owned. (See IRS Publication 550, *Investment Income and Expenses*.)

Nontaxable Dividends

Shareholders of C corporations may receive a return of capital or a tax-free dividend of more shares of stock or stock rights. These dividends are not treated the same as ordinary dividends or capital gain distributions.

Return of Capital

A return of capital is a dividend that is not paid out of the earnings and profits. It is a return of the investment that shareholders made in the stock of the firm. A return of capital is a reduction in the basis of the capital assets held by the C corporation. It also reduces the shareholder's basis in the stock. It is not taxed until the basis in the stock is fully recovered—then is taxed as long-term or short-term capital gain depending on how long the shares were held.

Stock and Stock Rights

Distributions by a C corporation of its stock to shareholders are known as stock dividends. Stock rights (also known as "stock options") are distributions of rights to acquire the corporation's stock. Generally, stock dividends and stock rights are not taxable. Business owners should carefully study IRS Publication 550, *Investment Income and Expenses*, and consult with tax and legal professionals before issuing stock dividends or stock rights. One miss step and the dividends may become fully taxable to the recipient shareholders.

☑ *Note*: Profits paid to S corporation shareholders are not dividends. A shareholder's pro rata interest in an S corporation's earnings are not subject to SE tax, even though the amount is included in the shareholder's gross income for tax purposes. The payments that an S corporation shareholder receives in the form of a reasonable salary are subject to withholding of payroll taxes (social security and Medicare taxes) but not SE tax. As long as the shareholder receives a reasonable salary, any additional distributions the shareholder receives are not taxable.

Draws

A draw is the removal of funds from a business by an owner. The tax ramifications of a draw are entirely determined by the legal form of the business.

Sole Proprietorships, Partnerships, LLCs

☑ Self-employed individuals—i.e., sole proprietors, partners in a partnership, or members (owners) of LLCs that are taxed as partnerships—cannot be employees of the businesses that they own. This is an often misunderstood point of law. The underlying principle is that you cannot hire yourself as an employee, pay yourself a wage, and deduct the payments as a business expense.

However, a self-employed individual may pay himself (withdraw funds) as much or as little money as he wants. The draw is not a wage. The business does not pay payroll taxes on it, nor can the business claim it as a tax deduction. The profit of the business, which is computed without regard to draws, is the business owner's wage. This amount is subject to SE taxes and must be included in the owner's personal Form 1040 tax return.

C Corporations

☑ Funds that an owner of a C corporation withdraws from his business must be classified as either employee wages or dividends. The wages are subject to payroll taxes and they are tax deductible to the C corporation. (See Employees' Pay.) Any amounts withdrawn from the business in excess of wages are classified as dividends. Dividends are not tax deductible and are generally taxable to the owner / shareholder. (See Dividends.)

S Corporations

☑ A shareholder's pro rata interest in an S corporation's earnings are not subject to SE tax, even though the amount is included in the shareholder's gross income for tax purposes. The payments that an S corporation shareholder receives in the form of a reasonable salary are subject to withholding of payroll taxes (social security and Medicare taxes) but not SE tax. As long as the shareholder receives a reasonable salary, any additional distributions the shareholder receives are not taxable.

Example

Joe Smith owns and operates a small plumbing partnership. Joe finds himself in need of cash to pay off a balloon payment on his residence. He draws $25,000 from the partnership. The partnership may not deduct the $25,000 as a business expense. Joe's Form 1040 tax filing will be based on his share of the partnerships profits irrespective of the $25,000 draw.

Education

There are basically two separate categories for business education expenses:

1. Education Assistance Programs
2. Work-Related Education and Training

☑ Education is one of those areas where tax-wise business owners need to pay particular attention. They may want to provide educational benefits and cover work-related education and training expenses for their employees and also participate in these programs themselves.

Education Assistance Programs

Employers may pay employees up to $5,250 annually as an education assistance benefit for non-job related education expenses. This amount is deductible to the employer and is not taxable to the employee. Any amounts in excess of $5,250.00 are considered wages paid to the employee. (See IRS Publication 15-B, Section 2, *Educational Assistance*.)

To qualify as a tax-free educational assistance program, the plan must be in writing and offered only to employees, i.e.,

- ☐ Current employees
- ☐ Former employees who retired, left on a disability, or were laid off
- ☐ Full-time leased employees with at least one year of service
- ☐ Business owners who are sole proprietors
- ☐ Partners who perform services for partnerships

All of the following tests must also be met for the educational assistance program to qualify in 2016:

- [ ] Eligibility rules cannot favor highly compensated employees, i.e., for individuals that are either:
- [ ] 5% or greater owners at anytime during the year or preceding year, or
- [ ] Paid more than $120,000 for the preceding year;
- [ ] The program cannot provide more than 5% of its benefits to individuals that own more than 5% of the stock, the capital, or profits interest of the business;
- [ ] Employees cannot choose to receive cash or other taxable benefits instead of educational assistance;
- [ ] Eligible employees must be given reasonable notice of the program.

Benefits can be used to pay for tuition, fees and similar expenses, books, supplies, and equipment. The payments may be for undergraduate- or graduate-level courses. Educational assistance benefits do not have to be for work-related courses; however, they cannot include payments for the following items:

- [ ] Meals, lodging, transportation, or tools or supplies (other than textbooks) that the student can keep after completing the course of instruction;
- [ ] Education involving sports, games, or hobbies—unless they are reasonably related to the business of the employer or are required as part of a degree program.

If your company doesn't have an educational assistance plan, or you provide an employee with assistance exceeding $5,250, you must include the value of these benefits as wages, unless the benefits are working condition benefits. Working condition benefits may be excluded from wages. Property or a service provided is a working condition benefit to the extent that if the employee paid for it, the amount paid would have been deductible as a business or depreciation expense.

Work-Related Education and Training

Businesses can deduct the expenses paid or reimbursed for the qualifying education and training of their employees. (See IRS Publication 970, *Tax Benefits for Education*.) To qualify it must meet at least one of the following two tests:

- ☐ The education must serve a bona fide business purpose and be required by the employer or the law for the employee to keep his or her present salary, status, or job.
- ☐ The education maintains or improves the skills needed by the employee to do his or her present work.

However, even if the education and training meet one or both of the above tests, it is not qualified if it:

- ☐ Is needed to meet the minimum educational requirements of the employee's present trade or business;
- ☐ Is part of a program of study that will qualify the employee for a new trade or business.

Employers deduct the cost of qualifying job-related education expenses for their employees on their business expense schedules. Employees do not have to include the paid or reimbursed job-related education expenses in their income.

In general, business owners can deduct the cost of their personal education if they can prove that the courses maintain or improve the skills that they need to run their present businesses. However, business owners cannot deduct the cost of any education that would qualify them for a new trade or profession—even if it also improves the skills that they need for their current line of work.

Tax Court Examples

A psychiatrist was allowed to deduct costs of studying to become a psychoanalyst since that was regarded as upgrading her skills.

A computer repairperson with no college degree who entered college to become a computer programmer could not claim an education deduction because he was taking classes to qualify for a new occupation.

Example

Joe Smith owns and operates a computer software company. Joe's full-time accountant, Bill, takes an accounting class at the local community college to improve his knowledge of accounting. The cost of the class is $6,000. Joe may deduct the entire amount because the class is for job-related educational purposes.

Alternatively, Joe's secretary, Sarah, takes the same accounting class at a cost of $6,000. Since accounting is not part of her job description, Joe may only deduct $5,250 as an education assistance benefit. Sarah must include the remaining $750 in income (the excess between the $6,000 paid and the $5,250 tax-free benefit allowed).

Employees' Pay

Employers can generally deduct the pay given to employees for services they perform for their businesses. The pay may include wages, salaries, vacation allowances, bonuses, commissions, and fringe benefits. And, the actual form of the pay may be in cash, property, or services. (See IRS Publications 15, *Circular E, Employer's Tax Guide*; 15-A, *Employer's Supplemental Tax Guide*; and 15-B, *Employer's Tax Guide to Fringe Benefits*.)

Wages paid by business owners to non-family employees are subject to federal and state taxes, including social security, Medicare, and federal unemployment (FUTA) tax. Income taxes are paid by each employee based on that individual's current tax rate. (See these sections in this chapter: Family Employees and Taxes.)

To be deductible, employees' pay must be an ordinary and necessary expense to the business. In addition, the payment to the employee must be reasonable and for services that the employee actually performed (IRC §162). The IRS will consider the following items and any other pertinent facts to determine if pay is reasonable:

Duties	Productivity
Responsibility	Task complexity
Time required	Cost of living

Abilities	Achievements
Comparative pay	Pay policies
Pay history	

The reasonableness question is particularly important to C corporations because of the way that they are taxed.

Review: The profits of a C corporation are taxed at the corporate level, and the dividends and other distributions made to the owners (shareholders) are not tax deductible against corporate profits. Therefore, dividends are subject to double taxation—at the business level and again at the shareholder's level.

The temptation for a C corporation (and LLCs that elect to be taxed as C corporations) is to pay very high wages to employees who are major shareholders. Since wages are tax deductible to the business, the amounts paid as wages to employee shareholders is actually taxed only once—at the personal level, thus avoiding double taxation. However, if the IRS determines that a salary to an employee shareholder is unreasonably high, the excessive part of the salary cannot be deducted by the C corporation and will be reclassified as an ordinary (taxable) dividend. (See these sections in this chapter: Dividends, Draws, and Taxes.)

☑ *Note*: Closely held C corporations should avoid issuing dividends unless absolutely necessary. Seek the advice of a competent accountant or attorney.

☑ Self-employed individuals—i.e., sole proprietors, partners in a partnership, or members (owners) of LLCs that are taxed as partnerships—cannot be employees of the businesses that they own. However, a self-employed individual may pay himself (withdraw funds) as much or as little money as he wants. The withdrawal is not a wage, the business does not pay payroll taxes on it, and the business cannot claim it as a tax deduction. The profit of the business, which is computed without regard to withdrawals, is the business owner's wage. This amount is subject to SE taxes and must be included in the owner's personal Form 1040 tax return. (See these sections in this chapter: Draws and Taxes.)

☑ As discussed earlier under the section discussing Draws, a shareholder's pro rata interest in an S corporation's earnings are not subject to SE tax, even though the amount is included in the shareholder's gross income for tax purposes. The payments that an S corporation shareholder receives in the form of reasonable compensation are subject to withholding of payroll taxes (social security and Medicare taxes) but not SE tax. As long as the shareholder receives reasonable compensation, any additional distributions the shareholder receives are not taxable.

There is an incentive to not pay much, if any, salaries to shareholder-employees to avoid the imposition of FICA and FUTA taxes.

Example

Joe owns and operates ABC Plumbing, Inc. (ABC) which has seven employees, including Joe. ABC is a C corporation and pays its employees every other week. The salaries and wages ABC pays to employees are tax deductible as long as they are reasonable. If ABC pays Joe an unreasonably large salary, the excessive amount above a reasonable salary for Joe's services would be reclassified as a dividend that is not tax deductible to ABC.

Entertainment

A business can deduct an entertainment expense only if the expense is both ordinary and necessary and meets one of the following two tests:

The entertainment expense was directly related to business (directly related test). This means that:

- ☐ The main purpose was the conduct of business
- ☐ The parties engaged in business during the event
- ☐ The parties expected a specific future business benefit

The entertainment expense was associated with a business activity (associated test). This means that it was:

- ☐ Associated with the active conduct of business
- ☐ Directly before or after a substantial business discussion

Entertainment includes any activity generally considered to provide entertainment, amusement, or recreation. Examples include entertaining guests at nightclubs, at social, athletic, and sporting clubs; at theaters; at sporting events; on yachts; or on hunting, fishing, vacation, and similar trips. Entertainment also includes the cost of meals (food, beverages, taxes, and tips) provided to a customer or client.

Businesses cannot deduct dues (including initiation fees) for memberships in any club organized for business, pleasure, recreation, or other social purposes. This includes dues paid to country clubs, golf and athletic clubs, airline clubs, hotel clubs, and clubs operated to provide meals in an atmosphere that is conducive to business discussions.

Typically, an employer can deduct only 50% of any otherwise deductible business-related entertainment expenses. This 50% deduction limit applies to reimbursements made to employees for expenses they incur for entertaining business customers as well as for costs incurred in entertaining clients on business premises, at a restaurant, or another location. The 50% limit also applies to expenses incurred at a business convention or reception, business meeting, or business luncheon at a club. (See IRS Publications 463, *Travel, Entertainment, Gift, and Car Expenses*, and 535, *Business Expenses*, Chapter 11.)

The IRS tends to scrutinize entertainment expenses. Therefore, it is advisable that the related expense be claimed in a different tax-deductible category if possible. Of course, the expense has to legally fit within the other category such as a promotion (advertising) expense. For instance, if an entertainment expense is for a business promotional activity or for a fringe benefit company party—this expense would be 100% deductible. (See Promotion (Advertising).) Through careful planning, wording of informational material, and event management, many entertainment-related expenses can be claimed as part of promoting the business and its products or services. These promotional expenses are often 100% deductible.

Example 1

Joe Smith owns a computer software company. Joe takes a potential client golfing, at a cost of $100, to discuss how his software would benefit the client's business. Joe may deduct $50 as a business expense for business entertainment purposes. The client is not required to include the round of golf as income.

Example 2

ABC Plumbing, Inc. (ABC) gives a holiday party for its employees. ABC leases the home of its president for the party at the fair market rate of $1,000. ABC also hires a caterer to prepare a buffet, purchases beer and wine, and hires bartenders through a temporary employment agency.

The event will not be taxable to the employees because the party qualifies as a de minimis fringe benefit. (See De Minimis Benefits.) The entertainment expenses (food preparation, beverages, and service) would be 50% deductible by the corporation. The $1,000 paid to the president will also be deductible to the corporation.

Family Employees

Payments made by business owners to family employees must be for services actually performed, and the amounts paid must be necessary, ordinary, and reasonable. (See Employee's Pay.) However, there are special rules for withholding and taxation that apply in various family employee situations. (See Taxes in this chapter and IRS Publication 15, *Circular E, Employer's Tax Guide.*)

For Example

Payments to a child under the age of 18 who works for his or her parents are not subject to social security and Medicare taxes if the business is a sole proprietorship or a partnership in which each partner is a parent of the child.

The wages for services of an individual who works for his or her spouse are subject to income tax withholding and social security and Medicare taxes, but not to FUTA tax.

The wages paid to a child or spouse are subject to income tax withholding as well as social security, Medicare, and FUTA taxes if he or she works for:

- ☐ A corporation, even if it is controlled by the child's parent or the individual's spouse;
- ☐ A partnership, even if the child's parent is a partner, unless each partner is a parent of the child;
- ☐ A partnership, even if the individual's spouse is a partner;
- ☐ An estate, even if it is the estate of a deceased parent.

The wages for services of a parent employed by his or her child are subject to income tax withholding and social security and Medicare taxes—however, they are never subject to FUTA tax, regardless of the type of services provided.

Fringe Benefits

According to IRS Publication 15-B, *Employer's Tax Guide to Fringe Benefits*, "A fringe benefit is a form of pay for the performance of service given by the provider of the benefit to the recipient of the benefit." In reality, most taxpayers know that a fringe benefit refers to things of value (over and above wages, salaries, commissions, and bonuses) that a business provides to owners and employees. However, a person who performs services does not have to be an employee—he may be an independent contractor, partner, or director.

Some taxpayers mistakenly assume that fringe benefits have some sort of a tax advantage to the recipient. That is, for the recipient, a fringe benefit might be tax-free, tax-deferred, partially taxable, or taxable at an advantageous rate. Over the years, tax laws have moved toward making all benefits to employees and owners taxable. In fact, any fringe benefit provided by an employer is taxable and must be included in the recipient's pay unless the law specifically excludes it. In other words, fringe benefits are taxable and become tax-free or tax-advantaged only if Congress grants a specific exception within the Code.

The following are examples of fringe benefits that are covered by tax exclusion rules that exclude all or part of the value of the benefit from the recipient's pay. (See IRS Publication 15-B, *Employer's Tax Guide to Fringe Benefits*.)

accident and health benefits	achievement awards
adoption assistance	athletic facilities
de minimis (minimal) benefits	dependent care assistance
educational assistance	employee discounts
employee stock options	group-term life insurance coverage
lodging on the business premises	meals
moving expense reimbursements	transportation (commuting) benefits
tuition reduction	working condition benefits

The secret of tax-wise business ownership is to focus on those fringe benefits that result in true "win-win" tax consequences, i.e., benefits (or a reimbursement for expenses) where both of the following occur:

- ☐ The recipient does not have to report the benefit or reimbursement on his tax return
- ☐ The business receives a tax deduction for the cost of the benefit or for the amount of the reimbursement

Example

Joe Smith owns XYZ Solutions, Inc. (XYZ), a computer software company with 150 employees. Mike Doe, an employee, receives reimbursement for two expenses that he paid on behalf of XYZ. The first reimbursement was for Mike's personal athletic membership at AB's Gym. XYZ reimbursed Mike for this expense because it was allowed under the company's employee fitness program. Mike's other claim was reimbursement of business mileage expenses that Mike incurred when he used his personal vehicle to visit one of XYZ's clients. (The mileage reimbursement request was submitted in compliance with the company's travel expense schedule.)

Taxation Consequences

XYZ cannot deduct the gym membership reimbursement because it is not an "ordinary and necessary" business expense that would otherwise be allowed under the Code. On the other hand, XYZ can deduct the business mileage expenses claimed by Mike. (See Vehicles.)

XYZ must include the reimbursement for the athletic membership on Mike's Form W–2. Mike must include the payment of gym dues as income on his personal tax return, but he will not have to include the reimbursement for the mileage expenses.

As this example shows, the Code grants tax exclusions based on the specific business-provided benefit. To make the situation even more complex, tax breaks for some fringe benefits are available only to one type of business organization, i.e., C corporations. This means that the owners and employees of sole proprietorships, limited liability companies, partnerships, and S corporations cannot deduct the expense of providing these specific benefits to their owners or employees.

Most business owners use fringe benefits as a partial offset to the inherent risks of engaging in business. Tax-wise business owners realize that fringe benefits are one of their most powerful tools in the creation of personal and estate wealth.

Furniture and Fixtures

See Office Furniture, Fixtures, and Equipment.

Home Office

The home office deduction is a deduction that business owners and certain employees can take for the cost of operating the business-use part of their homes. If the space qualifies and if a business owner has a net profit from his business, the home office deduction can lead to significant tax savings. (See IRS Publication 587, *Business Use of Your Home*.)

The home office deduction is separate from and in addition to deductions for everyday business expenses such as office supplies, legal fees, etc., and must be deducted from income after all other business expenses. It allows a deduction for mortgage interest, real estate taxes, gas, electric, water, garbage disposal, and home repairs based on the percentage of the home's area that qualifies as a home office. And, it also allows depreciation on the business portion of the home. However, business owners cannot use the home office deduction to show a business loss.

The advantage of the home office deduction is that it lowers net business income, which in turn lowers a business owner's adjusted gross income (AGI). Since several personal deductions are tied to AGI (limited to amounts over a percentage of AGI), the more AGI is legally reduced, the larger the allowed itemized deduction.

For business owners to claim this deduction the qualifying space must be used regularly and exclusively:

☐ As the taxpayer's principal place of business;

☐ As a place to meet or deal with patients, clients, or customers in the normal course of business or trade.

An employee may also be able to take a home office deduction if the use of the home is for the convenience of the employer and he or she is not renting the home office to the employer.

The Simplified Method

The IRS now provides a simplified method to determine expenses for business use of a home. It's an alternative to the calculation, allocation, and substantiation of actual expenses. In most cases, the deduction is arrived at by multiplying $5, the prescribed rate, by the area of your home used for a qualified business use. The area you use to figure your deduction is limited to 300 square feet.

If you elect to use the simplified method, you can't deduct any actual expenses for the business except for business expenses that are not related to the use of the home. You also can't deduct any depreciation (including any additional first-year depreciation) or section 179 expense for the portion of the home that is used for a qualified business use. The depreciation deduction allowable for that portion of the home is zero by the IRS for a year you use the simplified method. If you figure your deduction for business use of the home using actual expenses in a subsequent year, you will have to use the appropriate optional. When using the simplified method, the IRS instructs you to treat those business expenses related to the use of the home that are deductible as personal expenses, regardless if there is a qualified business use of the home, like mortgage interest, real estate taxes, and casualty losses, subject to any limitations.

The choice of whether to figure your deduction using the simplified method is made each taxable year. An election for a taxable year, once made, is irrevocable. (See IRS Publication 587, *Business Use of Your Home*. See also Revenue Procedure 2013-13, 2013-06 I.R.B. 478 and IRS Publication 946 for the optional depreciation tables.)

Independent Contractors

People who follow an independent trade, business, or profession in which they offer their services to the public (plumbers, auctioneers, lawyers, CPAs, etc.), are generally not employees. However, whether such people are employees or independent contractors depends on the facts in each case. As a general rule, an individual is an independent contractor if the person for whom the services are performed has the right to control or direct only the results of the work—but not the means and methods of accomplishing the results.

From a tax standpoint, independent contractors are not employees. A business does not withhold taxes, pay employment taxes, or file payroll tax returns on the fees paid to independent contractors. Because of this, tax professionals, lawyers, the IRS, and the entire court system have been arguing for years over who is or is not an independent contractor.

There are serious financial and legal risks to businesses that misclassify employees as independent contractors. If the IRS determines that some workers are employees rather than independent contractors—a business is immediately notified that back employment taxes and penalties are due.

☑ Businesses are permitted to take disputes over the employment status of workers to Tax Court. By doing this, a business prevents the IRS from assessing and collecting contested employment taxes and penalties while the dispute is still pending. Prior to this change in the law, a business that contested such a reclassification by the IRS had to first pay a major portion of the disputed tax, and then file a long and costly refund claim through the court system. Even if the IRS was proven wrong, many businesses failed before they could reclaim the disputed tax payments.

IRS Publication 15-A, *Employer's Supplemental Tax Guide*, Chapters 1 and 2, will help owners determine the employment status of workers who provide services to their businesses. If there is still some question after reviewing this document, owners can solicit the help of the IRS in determining whether a worker is an employee by filing Form SS-8, *Determination of Worker Status for Purposes of Federal Employment Taxes and Income Tax Withholding*.

Information Systems — Computers and Peripherals

The purchase or lease of information systems by a business is almost always an ordinary and necessary expense. The IRS classifies them in asset class 00.12, which includes computers and peripheral equipment used in administering normal business transactions and the maintenance of business records. (IRS Publication 946, Appendix B — *Table of Class Lives and Recovery Period.*)

Computers do not include adding machines, electronic desk calculators, accounting machines, copiers, and duplicating machines. These assets are in asset class 00.13 and may be depreciated over five to six years or claimed as a Section 179 deduction.

Peripheral equipment consists of auxiliary machines that are designed to be placed under the control of a computer. Non-limiting examples are card readers, printers, optical character readers, tape drives, disc drives, plotters, etc.

If the business leases these assets, the cost of a lease is recovered by amortizing it over the term of the lease. (See Rent — Lease Payments in this chapter and Amortization in Chapter 4.)

If the information systems are purchased:

☐ The cost may be recovered as a depreciation expense over five years (See Depreciation in Chapter 4 and IRS Publication 946, Appendix B, Asset class 00.12.)

☐ The business may opt to claim the entire cost in the year purchased as a Section 179 deduction (See Section 179 Deductions in Chapter 4 and IRS Publication 946, Chapter 2, *Electing the Section 179 Deduction*.)

☑ Information systems do not include computer software unless the software was bundled with the computer when it was purchased and the cost of the software was not separated on the invoice. In this case, the computer software must be included as an integral, inseparable part of the depreciation or Section 179 deduction claimed for the computer. (See Computer Software in this chapter and IRS Publication 946, *How To Depreciate Property*.)

Example

Joe Smith, owner of ABC Plumbing, Inc. (ABC), purchased a new computer and printer for his office administrator. The entire information system was priced as a unit and included the computer operating system and word processing software. ABC has the option of claiming the entire $5,000 as a Section 179 deduction in the year it was purchased. Alternatively, ABC may depreciate the $5,000 over five years.

Insurance

Liability and Malpractice Insurance

A business can deduct insurance premiums paid for protection against liability or wrongful acts on the job.

Life Insurance

Businesses may deduct premiums paid for group-term life insurance coverage for their employees provided that it meets all of the following conditions:

- ☐ It provides a general death benefit that is not included in the employee's income.
- ☐ It is provided to all employees or a group of at least 10 employees, whichever is less. (Shareholders of 2% or more of an S corporation's voting stock cannot be included as employees.)
- ☐ It does not favor key employees as to participation or benefits. (For 2016, key employees are officers

with annual pay of more than $170,000 and any individual with either 5% or more ownership in the business or 1% or greater ownership plus annual pay of more than $150,000.) (See IRC §416.)

☐ The amount of insurance is based on a formula that prevents individual selection by either the business or the employee.

☐ The business carries the policy (arranges for the payment of premiums).

A business can generally exclude the expense of all group-term life insurance coverage provided to an employee from that employee's wages subject to federal income tax withholding and FUTA tax. In addition, a business can exclude the cost of up to $50,000 of coverage from the employee's wages that are subject to social security and Medicare taxes.

Vehicle Insurance

See Vehicles.

Intangible Property

See Section 179 Intangibles.

Intellectual Property

Intellectual property such as copyrights and trademarks cannot be depreciated. Instead, the cost for these Section 179 intangibles must be amortized over 15 years. (See Section 179 Intangibles in this chapter, Amortization in Chapter 4, and IRS Publication 946, *How To Depreciate Property*.)

Licensing fees for the use of a trademark or copyrighted material are deductible in the year they are paid. (See Rent — Lease Payments.)

Example

Joe Smith owns a computer software company, ABC Soft, Inc. (ABC). ABC owns the copyright (with a basis of $75,000) to a speech recognition computer program. Each year for 15 years ABC may claim a Section 179 amortization deduction of $5,000 until the basis of the copyright is fully amortized ($75,000 divided by 15 years = $5,000 per year).

Interest — Loans, Mortgages, and Credit Cards

Businesses can generally deduct all interest paid or accrued during the tax year on debts that are related to their trade or business. The interest expenses are related to the trade or business if the underlying loan was used (or will be used) to pay trade or business expenses—regardless of what type of property or personal guarantee secures the loan. However, a business can deduct interest on a debt only if all the following requirements are met:

☐ The business or the business owners are legally liable for repayment of the principal and interest on the debt.

- ☐ The business (and/or business owner) and the lender must both fully intend that the debt will be repaid.

- ☐ The business and the lender must have a true debtor-creditor relationship, such as:

  - A written and fully executed loan agreement or promissory note with the creditor (even if the creditor is the business owner)
  - Terms that require the payment of a fair market interest rate

Example

ABC Plumbing, Inc. (ABC) decides that it is time to promote its products and services on the Internet. ABC seeks a loan from EFG Bank Corporation to pay consultants to establish ABC's Internet website. The loan ABC receives is for $100,000 at 10% interest, payable over a period of 15 years. ABC will be able to deduct the consultant fees and the interest it pays on the loan—and ABC will not be taxed on the $100,000 it received.

Internet — Access and Online Service Fees

A business can deduct all costs associated with the business use of the Internet. For home office situations where the services are used partly for business and partly for pleasure, only the pro rata portion of online time used for business is deductible. In this case, it will be necessary to keep a log recording the amount of business time spent online and the associated charges.

Leases

See Rent — Lease Payments.

Licenses

Licenses, registrations, and other fees assessed to allow a business to operate are deductible. This may include fees that are assessed against employees so that they are allowed to conduct the activities of the business.

> *Example*
>
> Joe Smith owns and operates a small plumbing business. Each year, Joe must pay a $200 license fee to the state for the privilege of doing business as a plumber within the state. Joe may deduct 100% of the license fee as a business expense.

Manufacturing Equipment

See Production (Manufacturing) Equipment.

Materials and Supplies

The cost of materials and supplies that are used in a trade or business is deductible as long as each expense is an ordinary and necessary requirement for that type of trade or business.

Example

Joe's Plumbing buys $1,500 worth of pipe and plumbing supplies at a local hardware store. While in the store, Joe also purchased a *Create Your Own Birdhouse Kit* for $100. The $1,500 for pipe and plumbing supplies would be 100% deductible; however, the birdhouse kit would not because it is not ordinary and necessary for the plumbing business.

Meals

Meal costs (amounts spent on food, beverages, taxes, and tips) are deductible when:

- ☐ The meals qualify as entertainment expenses—50% deductible (See Entertainment in this chapter and IRS Publication 463, *Travel, Entertainment, Gift and Car Expenses*.)
- ☐ The meals are a qualified employee fringe benefit—100% deductible (See IRS Publication 15-B, *Employer's Tax Guide to Fringe Benefits*.)
- ☐ The meals are consumed while traveling away from home on business—50% deductible (Higher deductibility is allowed for individuals who are subject to the Department of Transportation's "hours of service" limits, see IRS Publication 463.)
- ☐ The meals are provided as samples available to the public—100% deductible as a cost-of-goods-sold or as a promotional expense (See Promotion (Advertising) in this chapter and IRS Publication 535, *Business Expenses*.)

Entertainment Expense Meals

For the cost of a meal to be deductible as an entertainment expense the meal must be either directly related or associated with the active conduct of business. (See Entertainment.) The meal deduction is subject to a 50% limit unless the expenses meet one of the following exceptions:

1. The employee was reimbursed for the meal under an accountable plan—100% deductible. (See IRS Publication 463, Chapter 6.)
2. Meal costs are 100% deductible for self-employed taxpayers if:
   - The meal costs were incurred as an independent contractor (See Independent Contractors);
   - The expenses were reimbursed by a client or customer and included in income;
   - Adequate records of the expense are provided to the client or customer.
3. The meal was provided to the public as a means of advertising or promoting goodwill in the community.
4. The business actually sells meals to the public.
5. The meal is included in a package deal that includes a ticket to a qualified charitable event.

Fringe Benefit Meals

Businesses may deduct the cost of fringe benefit de minimis meals or meal money provided to employees. (See De Minimis

Benefits in this chapter and IRS Publication 15-B.) The deduction applies to:

- ☐ Coffee, doughnuts, or soft drinks
- ☐ Occasional meals or meal money provided to enable an employee to work overtime
- ☐ Occasional parties or picnics for employees and their guests

A deduction is also allowed for fringe benefit meals if they are furnished to employees on the business premises and provided for the convenience of the business, i.e., for a substantial business reason other than to provide the employee with additional pay. For example:

Emergency Call Availability
Meals furnished so that employees will be available for emergency calls that the business reasonably expects will occur during a meal period.

Short Meal Periods
Meals provided because the nature of the business restricts employees to a short meal period, and they cannot eat elsewhere in such a short period of time. For example, meals can qualify when the peak workload occurs during the normal lunch hour. But, if the reason for the short meal period is to allow the employee to leave earlier in the day, the meal will not qualify as a deduction.

Not Otherwise Available
Meals furnished because employees could not otherwise eat proper meals within a reasonable

period of time. For example, meals can qualify if there are insufficient eating facilities near the place of employment.

Food Service Employees

Meals furnished to restaurant or food service employees for the meal periods worked, if the meals are provided during, immediately before, or immediately after work hours. For example, if a waitress works through the breakfast and lunch periods, the employer can exclude from her wages (and deduct as a business expense) the value of the breakfast and lunch furnished in the restaurant for each day she works.

After Work Hours

Meals provided immediately after working hours that would have been furnished during working hours for a substantial non-pay business reason but, because of the work duties, were not eaten during working hours.

Inclusive Meals

All meals furnished to employees on the business premises if more than half of these employees are furnished meals for a substantial non-pay business reason.

Example

Joe Smith owns a plumbing company that specializes in emergency response services. The plumbers work 12-hour shifts and are on call the entire shift. The volume of emergency service calls is high. This makes scheduling adequate lunchtime breaks for employees almost impossible. Joe decides that it would be best for his business if he brings in lunch for his employees. The cost of the meals would be 100% deductible to Joe's business and a nontaxable fringe benefit to the employees.

Business Travel Meals

The cost of meals that are not reimbursed by clients or customers is generally 50% deductible when traveling away from home on overnight business trips. The cost of a meal must be reasonable (not lavish or extravagant) based on the facts and circumstances. The 50% limit can be figured using the actual cost of the meals or the standard meal allowance. (See http://apps.irs.gov/app/scripts/exit.jsp?dest=http://www.gsa.gov/perdiem IRS Per Diem Rates.[1]) The per diem rate is the highest amount that the federal government will pay its employees for lodging, meals, and incidental expenses (or meal and incidental expenses only) while they are traveling away from home in a particular area. The rates vary by location within the continental United States.

> *Example*
>
> Joe Smith works for ABC, Inc. as a traveling salesman. His employer gives him a corporate charge card for his meals. Joe incurred $300 worth of meals, taxes and tips. ABC, Inc. can deduct 50% of the value of the meals, taxes, and tips.

Promotional Meals

See Promotion (Advertising).

Office Furniture, Fixtures, and Equipment

The purchase or lease of office furniture, fixtures, and equipment by a business is almost always an ordinary and necessary expense. The IRS classifies these items in asset class 00.11—which includes such items as desks, files, safes, and communications equipment. (See IRS Publication 946, Appendix B — *Table of Class Lives and Recovery Period*.)

If the business leases these assets, the cost of a lease is recovered by amortizing it over the term of the lease. (See Rent — Lease Payments in this chapter and Amortization in Chapter 4.)

If the office equipment is purchased:

☐ The cost may be recovered as a depreciation expense over 7 to 10 years (See Depreciation in Chapter 4 and IRS Publication 946, Appendix B, Asset class 00.11.)

☐ The business may opt to deduct the entire cost in the year purchased as a Section 179 deduction (See Section 179 Deductions in Chapter 4 and IRS Publication 946, Chapter 2, *Electing the Section 179 Deduction*.)

Example

ABC Plumbing, Inc. (ABC) needed new office furniture. Joe Smith, president of ABC, purchased two chairs and a desk for $2,000. Rather than depreciate the cost, ABC chose to deduct the entire $2,000 as a Section 179 deduction in the year the furniture was purchased.

Office Services

It would be hard to imagine any business that does not need office services from time to time (telephone answering services, temporary secretarial services, etc.). Even business owners who work from home offices occasionally need to use conference rooms and professional office facilities to meet with clients and customers. The entire cost of these and most other office services is deductible if they are a necessary and ordinary part of conducting your type of business.

Example

Joe Smith opens "Joe's Internet Plumbing Advice, Inc." Joe sells advice over the Internet and travels all around the country in his Winnebago giving free seminars. Joe's home state has very high corporate and personal income tax rates. Because he is doing business over the Internet and nationwide, Joe decides to establish his business as a corporation in the State of Nevada. (Nevada does not collect corporate income taxes.) Joe hires a firm in Las Vegas, Nevada, to answer his Nevada business phone, receive faxes, forward mail, and provide an office and conference room on an as-needed basis. The costs for these services would be 100% tax deductible.

Postage

The cost of postage, special delivery services, a post office box, and other delivery services (excluding shipping and freight) incurred by a business are 100% deductible as long as they are reasonable, ordinary, and necessary expenses for the business. (See Shipping and Freight.)

Example

Joe owns and operates a small hot dog stand. He has no business mailing address, so he rents a post office box for his business. The rental fees that Joe pays will be tax deductible as an ordinary and necessary business expense.

Product Development

If a business has product development expenses, it should seek accounting and legal advice—because, depending on the situation, product development expenses may be:

- ☐ Currently deductible
- ☐ Eligible for special tax credits
- ☐ Capitalized and deducted over a period of at least five years

Production (Manufacturing) Equipment

Depending on the type of business, the purchase or lease of production (manufacturing) equipment is an ordinary and necessary business expense.

If the business leases the equipment, the cost of a lease is recovered by amortizing it over the term of the lease. (See Rent — Lease Payments in this chapter and Amortization in Chapter 4.)

If the production (manufacturing) equipment is purchased:

- ☐ The cost may be recovered as a depreciation expense over the useful life of the equipment (See Depreciation in Chapter 4 and IRS Publication 946, Appendix B — *Table of Class Lives and Recovery Periods.*)

- ☐ The business may opt to deduct the entire cost in the year purchased as a Section 179 deduction (See Section 179 Deductions in Chapter 4 and IRS Publication 946, Chapter 2, *Electing the Section 179 Deduction.*)

Example

ABC Slide, Inc. (ABC) manufactures residential swimming pool accessories, i.e., water slides. ABC needed a $35,000 automated tube-bending machine to increase its manufacturing capacity. ABC contacted XZ Capital Corporation (XZ), an equipment financing and leasing specialist. XZ offered ABC a five-year, open-end lease for $850 per month.

ABC studied the offer and discovered that the lease would cost $51,000 (60 months times $850). The upside for ABC was the monthly amortization deduction that it could claim ($850). The downside was that the lease was expensive given that the equipment would still have seven years of useful life remaining at the end of the lease (useful life of

12 years—asset class 39.0, IRS Publication 946, Appendix B).

ABC purchased the equipment for $35,000 and depreciated the cost over seven years as allowed by using the general depreciation schedule for asset class 39.0. After ABC fully recovered the $35,000 cost through depreciation deductions over the seven years, ABC could use the equipment without capital costs for the five years of remaining useful life. In addition, ABC would be able to write off as a current expense the interest on the loan to purchase the equipment. (See Interest — Loans, Mortgages, and Credit Cards.)

Promotion (Advertising)

Nothing will be sold until the market knows about the products or services offered by a business. Unfortunately, the market, whether local or international, is surprisingly difficult to reach, inform, and convince. The task of reaching and convincing customers to buy is called marketing. Whether the business is old or new or is introducing a product or a service, reaching and informing the marketplace is a major expense.

Marketing consists of two broad components—publicity and promotion.

1. Publicity is free "advertising" (such as press releases) that occurs when individuals or the media relay news about a business. There are no charges involved, but the business has no direct control of the process or the message. It is well

known that the very best, and most believable, publicity is by word-of-mouth. Unfortunately, without marketing, word-of-mouth will seldom succeed before bankruptcy sets in—especially if the business seeks regional, nationwide, or international markets.

2. Promotion includes: advertising, speeches, special events, direct mail, newsletters, brochures, on-hold tapes, and premiums (discounts), i.e., all marketing activities where the business being promoted controls the message.

The IRS realizes that marketing is essential to most businesses and it allows them to deduct reasonable promotional expenses. Obviously, the direct costs associated with the design, preparation, and delivery of mailers, catalogs, signs, and other promotional materials are deductible. The only gray area stems from the potential overlap between promotional expenses and entertainment expenses.

☑ A business owner may hold a promotional open house for existing and potential clients. If the event is classified as entertainment, the tax deduction is limited to 50% of the actual expenses involved in the open hours. If the tax-wise business owner claims the open house as an advertising expense, 100% of the costs are deductible. This area is a bit nebulous. Overuse and unreasonable claims for advertising expenses may flag the tax return for an audit. The business owner will then have to explain that the event "talked, walked, and looked like" promotion rather than entertainment.

Example

Joe Smith owns and manages a small plumbing business. He creates a small invitational flyer to a "Proper Plumbing Extravaganza." Joe plans to have the affair catered by Debbie's Pizza & Catering Service.

If Joe sends invitations to his close friends, employees, and key suppliers, the IRS would rule that the entire affair as entertainment and therefore only 50% deductible. However, Joe distributes the flyers throughout the local neighborhood. Since he made the affair available to the public, the IRS would be hard pressed to argue against Joe's claim that the event was a business promotional activity that is 100% deductible. The cost of the stationery supplies, printing, mailing list rental, stamps, and catering services is fully deductible.

For corporations, a schedule (including promotional expenses) that shows all corporation expenses must be attached to the corporation's tax return. The total corporate expenses from this schedule are reported as "other deductions" on line 26 of Form 1120 (U.S. Corporation Income Tax Return).

Property Improvements

See these sections in this chapter: Real Estate and Repairs.

Publications
— Business, Professional, and Trade

The cost of books and other publications that pertain to your business are tax deductible expenses. However, the cost of publications, periodicals, books, and other literature for personal use are not deductible unless they are allowed as an educational business expense. (See Education.) Publications such as professional journals, newspapers, and periodicals for the use of clients in waiting rooms are almost always deductible.

Example

Joe owns and operates a computer software company. Each day, in order to keep up with this rapidly advancing industry and to stay informed about his competitors, he has the *Wall Street Journal* delivered to his office. In addition, Joe has a book recommended by a popular book club delivered to his company each month, addressed to his attention. Joe had the books delivered to the office, because that is where he spends most of his time during the day. He reads them between meetings as a source of personal entertainment. Joe may deduct the full value of the newspaper as a business expense—but, he may not deduct the book club expenses because these publications have no legitimate business purpose.

Real Estate

Many businesses own the real estate (land and buildings) that is used in their trade or business. The cost of these real estate assets is a capital expense—i.e., costs that are added to (increase) the basis of a taxpayer's investment or non-depreciable property (capital asset).

The cost of any improvement that has a useful life of more than one year is added to the basis of real property. These include amounts spent to prolong the life of the property, increase its value, or adapt it to a different use. In addition, the following are examples of costs that increase basis:

- ☐ Extending utility service lines
- ☐ Legal fees for perfecting or protecting title, etc.
- ☐ Zoning costs
- ☐ Rehabilitation expenses (minus rehabilitation credits received, if any)
- ☐ Assessments for items that increase the value of the property such as paving roads

It is important to understand that real estate is a combination of the physical structures on land and the land itself. These two components of real estate are handled differently.

> Land can never be depreciated; however, if it is used for mining or logging, it can be depleted. (See IRS Publication 946, *How To Depreciate Property*.) Clearing, grading, and landscaping expenses are most often added to the basis of the land rather than depreciated.

Business real estate (except land, which is never depreciated,) is a depreciable capital asset that has a recovery period of 39 years. Certain specifically identified land improvement costs (landscaping, roads, etc.) are depreciable over 15 years. (See IRS Publication 946, *How To Depreciate Property*, and these sections in Chapter 4: Basis and Depreciation.)

Real estate developers must capitalize most pre-building improvement made to land, i.e. grading, utilities, streets, etc.

Example

Joe Smith owns a small plumbing business that has outgrown its current facilities. Responding to the situation, Joe builds a new building on land that he purchased earlier in the year. Starting with the tax year that the new building was constructed, Joe may claim a depreciation expense for the depreciable amount of the building. Joe may not deduct or depreciate the cost of the land—because land is not a depreciable asset.

Reimbursements

Employers often reimburse employees for business, education (See Education), and other expenses such as medical co-pays and deductibles. The reimbursements are important to employees because they must itemize these deductions on Schedule A of their Form 1040 income tax filings. This means that the deductions are limited to amounts that exceed 2% of the employee's adjusted gross income (AGI).

When an employer reimburses employees under an accountable plan:

- ☐ The employer can deduct 100% of the reimbursed expenses
- ☐ The reimbursement is not included as income on the employee's Form W-2

To qualify as an accountable plan:

- ☐ The employer's reimbursement arrangement must have a business connection—i.e., the expenses must be otherwise allowable business expense deductions;
- ☐ The employee must adequately account to the employer for his/her expenses within a reasonable period of time;
- ☐ The employee must return any reimbursement or allowance in excess of the expenses accounted for within a reasonable period of time.

(See IRS Publications 463, *Travel, Entertainment, Gift, and Car Expenses*, and 970, *Tax Benefits for Education*.)

Example

ABC Plumbing, Inc. (ABC), a C corporation, decides to adopt an accountable employee medical reimbursement plan. Under the plan, ABC will reimburse each employee for up to $10,000 annually for medical expenses. John is an employee of ABC and incurs the following medical expenses during the year

Insurance premiums:	$3,600
Co-pays:	$200
Deductibles:	$200
Total:	$4,000

John will receive the $4,000 reimbursement from ABC as a tax-free fringe benefit. ABC will be able to deduct the $4,000 as a business expense.

Note: Depending on the legal form of the business, the entire amount of the reimbursement may not be tax-free. The example was a C corporation which provides a 100% tax-free reimbursement to its employees.

Rent — Lease Payments

Rents (or lease payments) are amounts that are paid to use property in a trade or business that one does not own. In general, the cost of a lease for a business property, i.e., an auto lease, equipment lease, or building lease is recovered by amortizing it over the term of the lease.

Inclusions

- A business may generally include and deduct as rent amounts that it pays to cancel a business lease.
- If a business pays taxes to or on behalf of the lessor of property rented by the business, these taxes can be deducted as additional rent.

Fees paid to acquire an existing business lease on a property or equipment cannot be deducted. These costs must be amortized over the remaining term of the lease. For example, a business pays $10,000 to take over an existing 20-year lease for a building that has 10-years remaining before termination. The business must amortize this expense.

Restrictions

If the business has or will receive equity in or title to the property, the rent is not deductible.

The IRS may challenge rental deductions that it deems are unreasonably large. This issue usually arises if the entity claiming the deduction is somehow related to the lessor of the property. The test for reasonableness is that the rent paid to a related person must be the same as the FMV rent that would be paid to a stranger for the same property. Nonetheless, rent will not be considered unreasonable just because it is figured as a percentage of gross sales.

Only the portion of rent paid in advance by a trade or business that applies to the rented property during the tax year is deductible. The rest of the advance rent payment is deducted over the future tax periods to which it applies.

Payments that are claimed as rent but which are actually for the purchase of the property under a conditional sales contract are not deductible. In general, a conditional sales contract allocates some or all of the incremental payments for purchase of the property, or it transfers the property to the lessor for a nominal sum at a future date. (See IRS Publication 535, *Business Expenses*.)

Repairs

The cost of repairing or improving property that is used in a trade or business is either a currently deductible expense or a capital improvement. This can typically be deducted over a period of time as a depreciable expense. A business can deduct repairs that keep the property in a normal and efficient operating condition, as long as the repairs do not add to its value or usefulness or appreciably lengthen its useful life. All other repairs are capital improvements and must be depreciated. (See Depreciation in Chapter 4 and IRS Publications 535, *Business Expenses*, and 946, *How To Depreciate Property*.)

The cost of repairs includes the costs of labor, supplies, and certain other items. Examples of deductible repairs include:

☐ Patching and repairing floors
☐ Repainting the inside and outside of a building
☐ Repairing roofs and gutters
☐ Mending leaks

Example

Joe Smith owns and operates a small plumbing business. Joe purchases new brakes and a shiny new paint job for his work truck. Joe may deduct the entire amount of the brake job as a repair expense because it does not add value to the vehicle. On the other hand, Joe may only deduct the depreciable amount of the paint job over a 60-month period because the value of the vehicle increased as a result of its improved appearance.

Royalties

A "royalty" is compensation for the use of property—usually copyrighted material, patents, or natural resources. The royalty is the share of the product or profit derived from the property that is reserved by the owner for permitting another to use the property. If royalties are paid to the owners, developers, or patent holders in the ordinary course of operating a trade or business, the expense is deductible as a business expense. As with all business expenses, the cost must be ordinary and necessary, and it must be itemized in the business expense records.

Example

Joe Smith owns a computer hardware franchise to sell and service computers manufactured under the trademark name of ABC Computers (ABC). Joe pays ABC a franchise fee of $20,000 a year. This allows Joe to use the name and operate his business as ABC Computers. For the use of the trademarked ABC name, Joe may deduct 100% of the cost of the franchise fee as a royalty expense.

Scholarships

See Education.

Section 179 Intangibles

Certain intangible capitalized costs of "Section 179 intangibles" must be amortized over 15 years. (See IRS Publication 535, *Business Expenses*, Chapter 8.) These include the following types of property acquired after August 10, 1993:

- ☐ Franchises, trademarks, or trade names
- ☐ Noncompete agreements

The following properties, but only if they were obtained with the acquisition of assets that constitute a trade or business:

- ☐ Goodwill
- ☐ Patents and copyrights
- ☐ Client lists
- ☐ Design, patterns, and formats, including certain computer software

Seminars

The deductibility of seminars is somewhat confusing as shown by comparing the wording in two IRS Publications.

> IRS publication 550, *Investment Income and Expenses*, Chapter 3, *Nondeductible Expenses*, states: "You cannot

deduct expenses for attending a convention, seminar, or similar meeting for investment purposes."

However, IRS Publication 970, *Tax Benefits for Education*, under Qualifying Work-Related Education states the following:

> You can deduct the costs of qualifying work-related education as business expenses. This is education that meets at least one of the following two tests.
>
> 1. The education is required by your employer or the law to keep your present salary, status, or job. The required education must serve a bona fide business purpose of your employer.
> 2. The education maintains or improves skills needed in your present work.

However, even if the education meets one or both of the above tests, it is not qualifying work-related education if it:

- ☐ Is needed to meet the minimum educational requirements of your present trade or business, or
- ☐ Is part of a program of study that will qualify you for a new trade or business.

You can deduct the costs of qualifying work-related education as a business expense even if the education could lead to a degree.

If there is a sound business reason for attending a seminar or other short-term course, you can generally deduct the costs. (See Education.) If you have to travel to get to the seminar and the majority of your trip is spent attending the seminar, you can also deduct your travel costs as a business expense. (See Travel.) If, however, you spend more time on personal activities than attending the seminar, your travel expenses would be disallowed, but the seminar cost would be allowed.

☑ If you plan to attend seminars overseas or on a cruise ship, be sure you understand all the rules governing deductibility of your trip before you make the arrangements. Otherwise, expense deductions could be denied. (See IRS Publication 463, *Travel, Entertainment, Gift, and Car Expenses* and these sections in this chapter: Conventions, Education, Meals, and Travel.)

Example

Joe Smith starts an investing company. He decides to attend a three-day investment seminar costing $5,000. Unfortunately, Joe may not be able to deduct this expense unless he is an employee of his investing company and the seminar serves a bona fide business purpose.

Assume instead that Joe Smith went to work for JS Business and Asset Management, Inc. (JSBM) and that JSBM paid for the seminar to improve Joe's skills, the entire $5,000 would be a tax deduction for JSBM.

Figure 12-1. **Does Your Work-Related Education Qualify?**

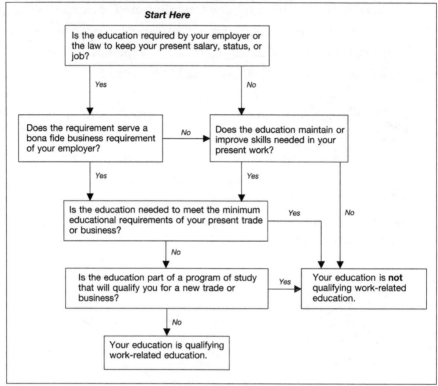

Shipping and Freight

Shipping and freight refers to costs that are associated with the transport of merchandise. The transport costs attributable to goods that a business sells are typically 100% deductible. The question of deductibility of the shipping and freight costs involved in receiving property is more complex.

If the received property is placed into or used to manufacture inventory that will be sold to customers—the delivery cost is added to the basis of inventory to be sold.

If the received property is a capital business asset—the costs of delivery are added to the basis of the asset and deducted over time as a depreciation expense.

Example

Joe Smith owns and operates a plumbing company. Joe purchases a heavy duty, 250-foot sewer snake for $2,500 that he plans to mount on one of his service trucks. The same supplier also shipped Joe a toilet for resale. The shipping costs were $250 for the snake and $25 for the toilet. For the snake, Joe must add the $250 delivery cost to the $2,500 purchase price and depreciate the $2,750 over the useful life of the asset. For the toilet, Joe must add the $25 to the basis of the toilet. Upon the sale of the toilet, Joe subtracts the basis of the toilet (cost-of-goods-sold) from the sale price to determine his profit from the sale. None of the delivery costs are currently deductible; however, the delivery cost of the snake is a depreciable business expense.

Stock Options

There are three classes of stock options:

1. Incentive stock options
2. Employee stock purchase plan options
3. Nonqualified (nonstatutory) stock options

☑ Generally, for income tax purposes, incentive stock options and employee stock purchase plan options are excluded from wages—both when the options are granted and when they are exercised. However, the spread (the FMV of the stock at exercise minus the exercise price) is included in wages subject to social security, Medicare, and FUTA taxes when the options are exercised. Income tax withholding is not required at the time of exercise. (See IRC §421, §422, and §423.)

☑ The spread on nonqualified options normally is included in wages for income tax purposes when the options are exercised. (See IRC §1.83-7, §421, §422, and §423.)

Supplies

See Materials and Supplies.

Tax Credits

Tax credits should not be confused with tax deductions. A tax deduction is an item of expense that reduces taxable business profit. A tax credit, by comparison, reduces taxes directly, on a dollar-for-dollar basis. For example, a tax deduction of $100 in a 28% tax bracket will save $28 in taxes. A tax credit of $100 will save $100 in taxes—regardless of the tax bracket.

Congress uses tax credits as special incentives to stimulate the economy or to encourage businesses to act in socially or environmentally responsible ways. Businesses need to do their own research because tax credits come and go—available one year and gone the next. (See IRS Publication 334, *Tax Guide for Small Business*, Chapter 4, for a list of current tax credit programs.)

Tax Penalties

Tax penalties are not deductible.

Taxes

Business owners and employers are responsible for collecting various state and federal taxes and remitting these to the proper agencies. In addition, they are required to pay certain taxes themselves.

Alternative Minimum Tax (AMT)

The alternative minimum tax (AMT) is a tax calculation that often increases the tax burden to a business over what would be due under normal rules. It applies to certain C corporations that are economically profitable but have reduced their tax liabilities by claiming:

- ☐ Large depreciation deductions
- ☐ Loss carry forwards

Fortunately, the Code exempts a C corporation from the AMT if it has no more than $5 million in average gross receipts during the last three tax years. The exemption continues until its three-year average of gross receipts is more than $7.5 million. Avoiding the AMT can have a major impact on the after-tax profitability of smaller C corporations.

Example

C corporations that are subject to AMT rules are deterred from owning key-person life insurance on owner/employees because the proceeds from life insurance settlements are taxable income under AMT rules (even though insurance settlements are tax-exempt under normal rules). On the other hand, smaller C corporations that are exempt from the AMT rules can mitigate the impact of personnel losses by purchasing key-person policies on vital owner/employees. In addition, they can insure the lives of shareholders in order to use tax-exempt life insurance settlements to fund stock buyback agreements.

Payroll Taxes

Social security and Medicare are the two payroll taxes that are deducted from every employee's paycheck and remitted to the IRS by every employer. This pair of taxes is often called FICA (Federal Insurance Contributions Act) or OASDI (Old Age, Survivors and Disability Insurance), or simply social security.

Payroll taxes that employers pay on behalf of their employees, such as the matching portion of FICA, are fully deductible. However, payroll taxes withheld from employees' wages are not deductible because employers receive a deduction for the full wages paid to employees before deducting the withheld taxes. (See Employees' Pay.)

Example

Joe Smith works for ABC, Inc. (ABC) where he is paid a monthly salary of $2,500. ABC must withhold 7.65% of Joe's salary. It also must match that amount and submit the funds to the IRS for the social security portion of FICA taxes. The matching portion of the social security payments is tax deductible to ABC as is the salary paid to Joe.

☑ The payroll taxes that a business owner pays on his or her own wages are deductible only if the business is a C corporation, S corporation, or an LLC that has elected to be taxed as an S or C corporation.

☑ If the business is a sole proprietorship, partnership, or LLC that is taxed as a partnership—the business owner (or owners) are considered self-employed. All self-employed individuals must also pay a combined social security and Medicare tax—the self-employment tax (SE tax). However, unlike other payroll taxes, SE taxes are not directly deductible as a business expense, although a partial deduction is allowed on personal Form 1040 tax returns. (See Self-Employment Tax in this chapter and IRS Publication 334, *Tax Guide for Small Business*.)

Property Taxes—Inventory

Some states impose a property tax on inventory, called an inventory tax or floor tax. This tax is 100% deductible.

Property Taxes—Personal Property

Some states and municipalities impose a property tax on business assets such as equipment, furniture, and tools. This tax is known as a personal property tax—although the property is not personal property, it is business property. The word personal is used in this context to refer to property other than real estate that is owned by a business.

Personal property taxes are based on the assessed value of business assets other than real estate. It is important for business owners to examine this tax bill closely to make sure that it does not include assets that the business no longer owns. In addition, the assessed value of each asset should be carefully checked so that older assets are not overvalued.

Personal property taxes are 100% deductible.

Property Taxes—Real Estate

Property taxes on business real estate are deductible. However, prepaid property taxes cannot be written off until the tax year that they apply to.

In some cases, a business can choose to capitalize real estate property taxes instead of writing them off. Capitalization of these taxes means that the taxes are added to the cost of the real estate and depreciated along with the real estate. The result is a smaller write-off currently and a larger write-off in future years. Real estate developers that purchase land for future development must capitalize property taxes on these land purchases.

Business owners who qualify for home office deductions can deduct a percentage of their home property taxes. (See Home Office in this chapter and IRS Publication 587, *Business Use of Your Home*.)

Sales Tax

Sales tax that is paid on business equipment, depreciable assets, and vehicles are not deductible as a current expense. It should be added to the cost of the property and deducted as a Section 179 expense or depreciated over the life of the asset. (Refer to these sections in Chapter 4: Depreciation, Section 179 Deductions, and Amortization.)

Sales tax that is paid on materials, supplies, and similar purchases, is also not deducted as a separate expense. It is added to the cost of the items purchased, and the total is then deducted as a current business expense.

Sales tax collected from customers is usually included in gross income by most businesses and then deducted as a current business expense when paid to the taxing authority. The net effect on the balance sheet is zero.

Self-Employment Tax

Self-employment tax (SE tax) is a combined social security and Medicare tax for self-employed individuals. (See IRS Publication 334, *Tax Guide for Small Business*.)

Taxpayers are self-employed if any of the following apply:

1. They carry on a trade or business as a sole proprietor or an independent contractor.
2. They are members of a partnership that carries on a trade or business.
3. They are otherwise in business for themselves.

Limited Partners
>Limited partners are generally not subject to SE taxes. However, guaranteed payment received for services performed for the partnership are subject to SE taxes.

C Corporations
>Even if a taxpayer owns most or all of the stock of a C corporation, the income received as an employee or officer of the C corporation is not subject to SE tax.

Corporate Directors
>Fees received for performing services as a director of a corporation are subject to SE tax.

S Corporation Shareholder and Officer
>A shareholder's pro rata interest in an S corporation's earnings are not subject to SE tax, even though the amount is included in the shareholder's gross income for tax purposes. However, if the shareholder is also an officer of an S corporation and performs substantial services, the shareholder is an employee of the S corporation, and the wages the shareholder receives are subject to withholding of payroll taxes.

Limited Liability Companies
>Because LLCs can elect to be taxed as partnerships, C corporations, or S corporations, the rules for SE taxes follow the LLCs taxation election. Therefore, earnings that are distributed to members (owners) from LLCs that are taxed as partnerships are subject to SE tax.

SE Tax Rates and Maximum Net Earnings
The SE tax rate on net earnings in 2015 was 15.3% (12.4% for social security plus 2.9% for Medicare). All net earnings of at least $400 are subject to the Medicare part, and the maximum amount subject to the social security part (12.4%) in 2016 is $118,000.

Business owners cannot deduct the SE tax as a business expense. However, they can deduct half of their SE tax on line 27 of Form 1040. This deduction lowers adjusted gross income, but it does not affect the net earnings from self-employment or the SE tax.

Unemployment Insurance Tax

Employers are required the pay federal unemployment insurance (FUTA) for their employees and may also have to make payments to a state unemployment compensation or disability benefit fund. These unemployment and disability taxes are 100% deductible.

Self-employment income of sole proprietors, partners in partnerships, and members (owners) of limited liability companies is not subject to FUTA. However, if this income is subject to state unemployment compensation or disability benefit fund taxes, these taxes are 100% deductible.

Use Tax

Use tax is a state mandated reverse sales tax that some states levy on businesses that make out-of-state purchases. The use tax laws require the business buyer to pay sales tax directly to the state where the business buyer resides on purchases from out-of-state vendors (unless the purchases are for resale).

Unlike other sales taxes which are added to the cost of items when they are purchased—use taxes are 100% deductible. (See Sales Tax.) Because the use tax is paid after the fact, most businesses deduct use taxes directly as a business expense.

Note: The use tax discussed above is completely different from the deductible federal excise tax levied on truckers, which is called a Highway Use Tax.

Tools

Tools with a useful life of a year or less are deductible in the year that they are purchased. More expensive tools may be expensed under Section 179 in the year purchased or depreciated. (Refer to these sections in Chapter 4: Depreciation and Section 179 Deductions.)

Travel

Defining Business Travel

For tax purposes, business travel expenses are the ordinary and necessary expenses of traveling away from home for the taxpayer's business, profession, or job.

A clarification of "traveling away from home" is found in IRS Publication 463, *Travel, Entertainment, Gift, and Car Expenses*.

"You are traveling away from home if:

Your duties require you to be away from the general area of your tax home substantially longer than an ordinary day's work, and

You need to sleep or rest to meet the demands of your work while away from home.

This rest requirement is not satisfied by merely napping in your car. You do not have to be away from your tax home for a whole day or from dusk to dawn as long as your relief from duty is long enough to get necessary sleep or rest."

". . . Generally, your tax home is your regular place of business or post of duty, regardless of where you maintain your family home."

Deductions for travel-related business expenses that do not meet the IRS requirements for business travel are generally limited to transportation expenses (mileage allowance or actual expenses). (See Vehicles.)

Deductible Expenses

The type of business travel expenses that can be deducted depends on the facts and circumstances involved. The following are expenses that are deductible when a taxpayer travels away from home for business purposes. (For deductibility limits, refer to IRS Publication 463, *Travel, Entertainment, Gift, and Car Expenses*, and these sections in this chapter: Meals and Vehicles.)

Transportation
- ☐ Travel by airplane, train, bus, or car between the taxpayer's home and the business destination
- ☐ Fares for transportation between the airport or station and a hotel and between the hotel and locations where business is conducted

Baggage and Shipping
- ☐ Sending baggage, samples, or display material to and from temporary work locations

Autos
- ☐ Operating and maintaining a car when traveling away from home on business (actual expenses or standard mileage rate, plus business-related tolls and parking) (See Vehicles.)
- ☐ The business-use portion of rental car fees and expenses

Lodging and Meals
- ☐ Lodging and meals

Other
- ☐ Dry cleaning and laundry
- ☐ Business communications (telephone, fax, Internet, etc.)
- ☐ Tips associated with allowable business travel expenses
- ☐ Miscellaneous expenses related to business travel (stenographer's fees, computer rental, etc.)

Travel in the United States

All travel expenses are deductible if the trip is entirely business related. (For deductibility limitation and requirements, see IRS Publication 463 and the following two sections in this chapter: Meals and Vehicles.)

If the primary reason for the trip was for business purposes but personal side trips and activities were taken, only business-related travel expenses are deductible. These expenses include the travel costs of getting to and from the business destination and any business-related expenses at the business destination.

If a spouse, dependent, or other individual goes with a business owner (or his employee) on a business trip or to a business convention, the additional travel expenses are generally not deductible. However, the travel expenses are deductible if that person:

- ☐ Is your employee,
- ☐ Has a bona fide business purpose for the travel,
- ☐ Would otherwise be allowed to deduct the travel expenses.

Example

Joe Smith owns and operates a computer software company. Each year, Joe attends a three-day computer software conference in San Francisco. Knowing that his wife loves San Francisco, he brings her along for a second honeymoon. Joe attends meetings throughout the day but leaves his evenings open to spend with his wife.

Joe pays $285 a day for a double room. A single room costs $225 a day. Joe can deduct 100% of his airline ticket and business-related expenses but only $225 a day for his hotel room. The expenses for Joe's wife are not deductible because she is not Joe's employee and she is not in San Francisco for business purposes.

If the trip was primarily for personal reasons, such as a vacation, the entire cost of the trip is a nondeductible personal expense. However, expenses that a business owner has at the vacation destination that are directly related to his or her business are deductible.

Travel Outside of the United States

☑ There are special rules with regard to business travel outside the United States. Business owners are cautioned to review all of the rules governing deductibility before making plans for foreign business travel or to attend conventions overseas. Failure to properly plan a trip or to save all of the necessary documentation may mean that business travel deductions will be denied. (See IRS Publication 463, Chapter 1, *Travel*.)

Travel Entirely for Business

All travel expenses are deductible if the trip is entirely for business or considered entirely for business. A trip is considered entirely for business if:

- ☐ You are an employee and have no substantial control over the trip—self-employed individuals and major shareholders of small corporations do have substantial control;

- ☐ You were outside the United States for a week or less, combining business and nonbusiness activities;
- ☐ The trip was more than a week but you spent less than 25% of the total time on nonbusiness activities;
- ☐ You can establish that a personal vacation was not a major consideration, even if you have substantial control over arranging the trip.

Travel Primarily for Business

If travel outside the United States is primarily for business but time is spent on other activities (i.e., the trip is not considered entirely for business), expense deductions are limited to:

- ☐ The business portion of the cost of getting to and from the business destination
- ☐ Expenses incurred on business days while at the business destination

Business days include

- Any day spent traveling to or from a business destination
- Days required at a particular place for a specific business purpose (included even if most of the day is spent on nonbusiness activities)
- Days spent during working hours in pursuit of the trade or business (include days prevented from working because of uncontrollable circumstances)

- Weekends, holidays, and other necessary standby days if they fall between business days

Travel Primarily for Personal Reasons

The entire cost of travel outside the United States primarily for vacation or for investment purposes is a nondeductible personal expense. Normally allowable business expenses (i.e., education deduction for registration fees to attend brief professional seminars or continuing education programs) are still deductible—but not as business travel expenses.

Travel by Luxury Ocean Liner

Deductions for business travel by ocean liner, cruise ship, or other forms of luxury water transportation are limited to twice the highest federal per diem rate allowable at the time of travel. When meals and entertainment are separately stated on the billing, these amounts are subject to the 50% expense deduction limit. (See IRS Publication 463, Chapter 1, *Travel*, and these sections in this chapter: Entertainment and Meals.)

☑ The daily limit on luxury water travel does not apply to expenses to attend a convention, seminar, or meeting on board a cruise ship. (See Conventions in this chapter and IRS Publication 463, Chapter 1, *Travel*.)

Vehicles

Business owners can deduct the costs of operating a car, truck, or other vehicle in their businesses. These tax-deductible costs include gas, oil, repairs, license tags, insurance, and depreciation. However, only the portion of an expense that is directly attributable to the business use of the vehicle is deductible. For instance, regular commuting expenses and the costs associated with vehicle uses that the IRS considers personal in nature are not deductible. (See IRS Publication 463, *Travel, Entertainment, Gift, and Car Expenses*, Chapter 4, Transportation.)

Most businesses require the use of an automobile for the necessary and ordinary conduct of their commercial activities on at least a part-time basis. Many, depending on the type of business, require the use of a vehicle full time. Regardless of the amount of time a vehicle is used for business, owners have two ways to calculate the tax deduction for their business-related vehicle expenses. Taxpayers may deduct the actual costs of using the vehicle for business purposes or they may claim a per business-use mile standard deduction allowance.

Actual Expenses

Business owners may keep itemized records of all actual, business-related, vehicle expenses and claim a current tax deduction for these costs. Actual car expenses include the costs of:

Depreciation deduction	Garage rent
Gas	Insurance
Lease payments	Licenses
Oil	Parking fees
Registration fees	Repairs
Tires	Tolls

If the vehicle is used for both business and personal purposes, the taxpayer must divide expenses between these two uses. This is usually done based on the number of miles driven for each purpose. For example, if a vehicle is driven a total of 20,000 miles in a tax year and 15,000 of those miles are for business purposes, 75% of the actual car expense would be tax deductible (15,000 divided by 20,000 times 100% = 75%).

For some businesses, keeping itemized records of the numerous vehicle-associated expenses is a tedious task. They may prefer to use the optional standard mileage tax deduction allowance (Standard Mileage Rate).

Standard Mileage Rate

For 2015, the standard mileage allowance is 57.5 cents per mile, compared to 56 cents per miles in 2014 (in 2016, it is 54 cents per mile). The standard mileage rate is in lieu of depreciation and all vehicle expenses except parking, tolls, interest, and state and local taxes. Check IRS Publication 463, *Travel, Entertainment, Gift, and Car Expenses*, to find the standard mileage rate for the current tax year.

☑ If a taxpayer wants to use the standard mileage rate, he must choose to use it in the first year that the vehicle is available for business use.

☑ If a taxpayer wants to use the standard mileage rate for a leased vehicle, he must use it for the entire lease period.

The standard mileage rate cannot be used if a taxpayer:

- ☐ Uses the vehicle for hire
- ☐ Uses the vehicle in fleet operations
- ☐ Claims a depreciation or Section 179 deduction for the vehicle

Taxpayers must keep a record of the business purpose for the trip and the miles driven. Vehicle expenses must be prorated between personal and business uses.

Example

Joe Smith owns and operates a plumbing business. Joe has one employee, Mike Doe. Mike uses his personal truck for plumbing calls on behalf of Joe's plumbing business. In 2015, Mike spent $2,550 in actual costs to drive his truck 10,000 miles for Joe's business. Joe reimburses Mike at the standard mileage allowance of 57.5 per mile ($5,750). Joe is allowed to deduct 100% of the payment to Mike for the use of his truck. Mike is also allowed to deduct $5,750 by claiming the standard mileage rate when filing Form 2106, *Employee Business Expenses*, with his personal tax return.

An important difference between using the standard mileage rate and claiming actual expenses is the handling of depreciation. The standard mileage rate includes depreciation, regardless of the value of the vehicle, whereas actual expenses will not include depreciation once a vehicle is fully depreciated. This may be an incentive to keep older vehicles in service even after they are fully depreciated.

Example

Joe Smith owns and operates a plumbing business. The business owns a truck used for business purposes. Joe keeps meticulous records and deducts the actual expenses for operating the vehicle. These expenses include the depreciation deduction allowed by the IRS schedule as well as all out-of-pocket costs. Joe can continue to annually deduct his out-of-pocket costs for operating the vehicle, but the depreciation deduction will stop after the truck is fully depreciated.

In addition to using the standard mileage rate, taxpayers can deduct any business-related parking fees and tolls. For example, a taxpayer can deduct business-related parking fees when visiting a customer or client. However, parking fees paid at a taxpayer's principal place of work are considered nondeductible commuting expenses (IRC §162 controls this deduction).

Example

Joe Smith works for ABC Plumbing, Inc. (ABC). As part of his job, Joe travels regularly to local businesses to conduct repairs. ABC reimburses Joe 57.5 cents per mile plus parking expenses. These reimbursements are deductible to ABC and are nontaxable to Joe.

Vehicle Deduction Limits

Commuting

Typically, commuting expenses from a home to a business are not deductible. This includes taking a bus, carpool, trolley, subway, or taxi as well as driving any vehicle. However, a side trip to visit a client or customer on the way to a primary place of business is deductible. Traveling between two places of business is also deductible.

Fees paid to park at a taxpayer's principal place of business are nondeductible commuting expenses. However, parking fees when visiting a customer or client are deductible business-related expenses.

When an office in his home qualifies as a principal place of business, a taxpayer can deduct daily transportation costs between his home and another work location that is in the same trade or business. (To determine if a home office qualifies as a principal place of business, see IRS Publication 587, *Business Use of Your Home*.)

Fines

Fines paid for traffic violations are not deductible.

Loan Interest

Employees cannot deduct any interest paid on a vehicle loan even if the vehicle is used 100% for business. However, self-employed taxpayers who use a personal vehicle for business can deduct the portion of the interest expense for a vehicle loan that represents the business use of the car.

Section 179 Deduction

A Section 179 deduction can only be claimed in the year that the vehicle is ready and available for a specific use, whether a trade or business, a tax-exempt activity, a personal activity, or for the production of income. This means that a car first used by a taxpayer for personal purposes cannot qualify for a Section 179 deduction in a later year when its use changes to business. However, the taxpayer may be able to claim a business depreciation deduction.

To be eligible to claim a Section 179 deduction, a vehicle must be used more than 50% for business in the year it is acquired. The total amount of Section 179 and depreciation deductions that a taxpayer can claim for a vehicle is limited. For instance, these deductions were limited for vehicles placed in service in 2013 and later to not more than $3,360. The section 179 and depreciation deduction limit is reduced if the business use of the vehicle is less than 100%. For example, a 60% business use would limit the total Section 179 and depreciation deduction to $2,016 ($3,360 times 60% = $2,016).

The total amount you can elect to deduct for certain sport utility vehicles and certain other vehicles placed in service is $25,000.

Taxes—Luxury and Sales

Luxury or sales taxes on vehicles are not deductible. These taxes are part of the vehicle's basis and they are recovered through depreciation.

Table 2-1. **When Are Entertainment Expenses Deductible?**

General rule	You can deduct ordinary and necessary expenses to entertain a client, customer, or employee if the expenses meet the directly-related test or the associated test.
Definitions	<ul><li>Entertainment includes any activity generally considered to provide entertainment, amusement, or recreation, and includes meals provided to a customer or client.</li><li>An ordinary expense is one that is common and accepted in your trade or business.</li><li>A necessary expense is one that is helpful and appropriate.</li></ul>
Tests to be met	Directly-related test<ul><li>Entertainment took place in a clear business setting, or</li><li>Main purpose of entertainment was the active conduct of business, and You did engage in business with the person during the entertainment period, and You had more than a general expectation of getting income or some other specific business benefit.</li></ul>Associated test<ul><li>Entertainment is associated with your trade or business, and</li><li>Entertainment is directly before or after a substantial business discussion.</li></ul>
Other rules	<ul><li>You cannot deduct the cost of your meal as an entertainment expense if you are claiming the meal as a travel expense.</li><li>You cannot deduct expenses that are lavish or extravagant under the circumstances.</li><li>You generally can deduct only 50% of your unreimbursed entertainment expenses (see 50% Limit).</li></ul>

Note

1. Effective for 2012, the IRS no longer updates Publication 1542. Instead, current per diem rates are found on the Per Diem Rates page at the U.S. General Services Administration (GSA) website. Other information regarding per diem rates, such as substantiation methods and transition rules, are found in Publication 463, *Travel, Entertainment, Gift, and Car Expenses.*

CHAPTER

Tax Deferral

- ☐ Business-Sponsored Plans
- ☐ Individual Retirement Accounts
- ☐ Health Savings Accounts
- ☐ Health Reimbursement Arrangements

"Postponement: the sincerest form of rejection."

—ROBERT HALF

Even the most optimistic forecasters see trouble ahead for our social security system. In fact, few Americans truly believe that its benefits will provide enough money to see them through their golden years. Because of the pessimistic public opinion, social security has become a hot issue in our nation's Capitol. Rarely does a member of Congress miss a chance to give his or her spin on the situation. Regardless of the rhetoric, tax-wise business owners know that in order to fill the financial gap that social security was never designed to handle, they must create wealth accumulation through their own tax deferral plans.

☑ The purpose of this chapter is to provide tax-wise business owners with general information about the most beneficial tax deferral plans that they can set up for both their employees and themselves. However, this chapter does not contain all of the rules and exceptions that apply to each of these plans. Federal law heavily regulates this complex area, and Congress invariably adds new twists annually. Therefore, this is an area that definitely requires qualified professional help and guidance. Tax-wise business owners realize that the cost involved in setting up quality tax-deferral plans is a small price to pay in order to maximize the benefits of one of the best tax reasons for being in business.

Business-Sponsored Retirement Plans

Tax deferral plans that are set up and sponsored by businesses (employers and self-employed individuals) include the following types of retirement plans:

- ☐ SEP (simplified employee pension) plans
- ☐ SIMPLE (savings incentive match plan for employees) plans
- ☐ Qualified plans (also called H.R. 10 plans or Keogh plans when covering self-employed individuals)

All of these plans offer business owners and their employees a tax-favored way to save for retirement. Tax-favored in that:

- ☐ Employers can deduct contributions made to these plans for employees (including owner-employees);

☐ Sole proprietors can deduct contributions made for themselves;

☐ Trustees' fees can be deducted if contributions to the plan do not cover them;

☐ Earnings on the contributions are generally tax-free until they are distributed from the plan.

SEP Plans

Simplified employee pension plans (SEP plans) allow employers to contribute directly to a traditional individual retirement account (SEP-IRA) set up for each eligible employee. (Self-employed individuals can contribute toward their own SEP-IRA accounts.) Under SEP plans, contributions are made without employer participation which is involved in the more complex procedures required under qualified plans. Employers simply make contributions to the financial institution where each SEP-IRA is maintained. Each employee owns and controls his or her own SEP-IRA.

Set Up

There are three basic steps in setting up a SEP.

1. The SEP plans must be in writing.
2. Eligible employees must be informed about the SEP.
3. At a minimum, a SEP-IRA must be set up for each eligible employee.

Participation

Eligible employees must, at a minimum, include all individuals who meet all of the following requirements:

1. Attained age 21
2. Worked for the employer in at least three of the last five years
3. Received at least $550 in compensation from the employer for the year (subject to annual *cost-of-living adjustments* in later years).

☑ Employers can use less restrictive participation requirements than those listed above, but not more restrictive ones. (See IRS Publications 519, *U.S. Tax Guide for Aliens*, and 560, *Retirement Plans for Small Business*, for further clarification of eligible and excludable employees.)

Contributions

SEP-IRA contributions must be in the form of money (cash, check, or money order). They are deductible by the employer, within limits (as discussed later), and they are generally not taxable to the plan participants. Employers do not have to make contributions every year; however, if contributions are made, they must be based on a written allocation formula that does not discriminate in favor of highly compensated employees.

Contributions for 2015 to SEP-IRA accounts cannot exceed the lesser of 25% of the employee's compensation or $53,000 (subject to annual cost-of-living adjustments for later years). These limits also apply to contributions made to the SEP-IRA accounts of self-employed individuals. (See IRS Publication

560, *Retirement Plans for Small Business*, for special rules for figuring maximum deductible contributions.)

☑ If contributions are also made to a defined contribution plan, as discussed later in this chapter, compensation up to $265,000 (in 2015—subject to cost-of-living adjustments for later years) of an employee's compensation may be considered. This limit includes contributions to a SEP as well as contributions that are made to a defined contribution plan.

SIMPLE Plans

The unique feature of a savings incentive match plan for employees (SIMPLE plan) is that employees are allowed to make salary reduction contributions to the plan rather than receiving these amounts as a part of their regular pay.

Set Up

A SIMPLE plan can be adopted by employers with 100 or fewer employees who were paid $5,000 or more in the preceding year.

SIMPLE plans must be in writing and maintained on a calendar-year basis. They can be set up using either SIMPLE IRAs (SIMPLE IRA plans) or as part of a 401(k) plan (SIMPLE 401(k) plan).

SIMPLE IRA Plan

The SIMPLE IRA plan is adopted when the employer has completed all of the appropriate instructions on one of the SIMPLE plan documents (IRS *Form 5304–SIMPLE* Not for Use With a Designated Financial

Institution, or IRS *Form 5305–SIMPLE* for Use With a Designated Financial Institution). Employers have two ways to set up a SIMPLE IRA plan, they can:

1. Allow each plan participant to select the financial institution for receiving his or her contribution (by filing IRS *Form 5304–SIMPLE*)

or

2. Require all contributions to be initially deposited at one designated financial institution (by filing IRS *Form 5305–SIMPLE*)

SIMPLE IRAs are the individual retirement accounts or annuities into which contributions are deposited. A SIMPLE IRA must be set up for each eligible employee.

☑ *Note:* A SIMPLE IRA cannot be designated as a Roth IRA. Contributions to a SIMPLE IRA will not affect the amount an individual can contribute to a Roth IRA.

SIMPLE 401(k) Plan

Employers may adopt a SIMPLE 401(k) plan that generally satisfies the rules associated with qualified retirement plans as discussed later in this chapter.

Participation

Any employee who meets the $5,000 compensation threshold during any two years preceding the current calendar year (and is reasonably expected to meet this threshold during the current calendar year) is eligible to participate in the SIMPLE plan. Self-employed individuals who received earned income and owner-employees may also participate.

Contributions

Salary reduction contributions by each employee to a SIMPLE plan are limited to $12,500 in 2015 and 2016. The contribution limits will be adjusted for inflation in future years.

Participants age 50 or older may make additional contributions of $3,000 in 2015 or 2016, so the total contribution limit for a participant age 50 or older is $15,500. The catch-up contribution limits will also be adjusted for inflation in future years.

Employers must contribute to each employees account by either:

- ☐ Matching the employee's salary reduction contribution on a dollar-for-dollar basis up to a limit of 3% of the employee's compensation

  or

- ☐ Making a nonelective overall contribution of 2% of compensation on behalf of each eligible employee

All contributions to a SIMPLE account are fully vested immediately, and the employee's rights to any contributions are non-forfeitable. These contributions under a SIMPLE IRA plan are "elective deferrals" that count toward the overall annual limit on elective deferrals the employee can make to this and other plans permitting elective deferrals.

Qualified Plans

Most pension and profit sharing plans are qualified retirement plans. These are retirement plans that:

- ☐ Meet the requirement of the Employee Retirement income Security Act of 1974 (ERISA) and related federal tax laws
- ☐ Hold each employee's share of assets and earnings until the employee leaves the company or retires.

These plans must be for the exclusive benefit of employees or their beneficiaries. However, a qualified plan can include coverage for a self-employed individual. In this case, the self-employed individual is treated as both an employer and as an employee. Qualified retirement plans that are established by self-employed individuals were sometimes formerly referred to as Keogh or H.R. 10 plans.

☑ A sole proprietor, a partnership, or a limited liability company may establish qualified plans. However, an employee of these business entities, an individual partner of a partnership, or a member of an LLC cannot set up his or her separate qualified plan.

☑ Corporations (both C and S) can establish qualified plans. However, a shareholder of a corporation cannot establish his or her separate qualified plan.

Business owners usually receive an immediate deduction, subject to limits, for contributions made to qualified plans, including those made for their own retirement. The contributions (earnings and gains on them) are generally tax-free until distributed by the plan.

There are three types of qualified plans—profit-sharing plans, money purchase pension plans, and defined benefit plans. Employers can establish more than one qualified plan, provided that the contributions to all of the plans do not total more than the overall limits discussed later in this section.

Profit-Sharing Plan

A profit-sharing plan is designed to allow employees to share in the profits of the business. Each participant has an individual account into which the employer deposits contributions as defined under the plan. These amounts accumulate until the participant reaches a certain age, a fixed number of years of service, or upon certain other occurrences as defined in the plan. Although the name implies otherwise, contributions do not have to be made out of the net profits of the business.

The plan does not need to provide a definite formula for figuring the portion of profits that must be contributed by the employer. However, absent a set formula, the employer must make systematic and substantial contributions to the profit-sharing plan. Regardless of the contributions made to the plan, allocations among the participants and distributions of accumulated funds must be defined by set formulas. Benefits are determined by the size of the contributions and the earnings achieved on the funds prior to distribution.

In general, profit-sharing plans allow the employer more flexibility in making contributions than the other qualified plans—but the maximum deductible contribution may be less.

Money Purchase Pension Plan

Contributions to money purchase pension plans are fixed relative to a set formula that is based on a participant's compensation or various defined factors—other than business profits. The employer's contributions are required without regard to the profitability of the business (or to whether the self-employed person has earned income). Although contributions are fixed, benefits are determined by the size of the contributions and the earnings achieved on the funds prior to distribution.

Defined Benefit Plan

A defined benefit plan, as the name implies, is any qualified plan that requires contributions based on what is needed to provide a determinable benefit to a specific plan participant. Defined benefit plans typically require continuing professional assistance—they involve complex actuarial assumptions and computations to figure the contributions necessary to meet the benefit requirements for each participant.

☑ Unlike profit-sharing and money purchase pension plans, forfeitures under a defined benefit plan cannot be used to increase the benefits an employee would otherwise receive under the plan. Forfeitures must be used instead to reduce employer contributions.

Elective Deferrals — 401(k) Plans

All profit-sharing plans (and certain money purchase pension plans in existence prior to June 27, 1974) can include a cash or deferred arrangement or 401(k) plan. (See IRC §401(k).) Under these 401(k) plans, participants may choose to have part of their before-tax compensation contributed directly to the plan rather than received as taxable income.

Elective deferrals are made as a percentage of the employee's salary, up to a dollar limit of $18,000 in 2015. 401(k) contribution limits will be adjusted for inflation each year.

People 50 and older can contribute an additional $6,000 in 2015. The total contribution limit for people 50 and older is therefore $24,000.

Some companies match a portion of employee contributions and may also make additional contributions on behalf of their employees. These company contributions may be distributed according to the plan's vesting schedule. Employees who leave before they are fully vested may not receive all of the company's matching contributions. Self-employed taxpayers may also make deductible matching contributions to their 401(k) plans.

Employees do not pay taxes on their deferred 401(k) contributions until they receive distributions from the plan. The matching contributions to 401(k) plans made by employers are generally deductible to the employer and are tax-free to participants until distributed from the plan.

Roth 401(k) Plans

Since 2006 employers with 401(k) plans also have had the option of offering the Roth 401(k) plan. Contributions to a Roth 401(k) are made with after-tax dollars, but investment gains are tax-free. For 2015, the maximum an employee can contribute to all of his or her traditional and Roth IRAs is the smaller of:

- ☐ $5,500 ($6,500 if you're age 50 or older), or
- ☐ Your taxable compensation for the year.

Set Up

There are two basic steps in setting up a qualified plan:

1. The employer must adopt a written plan.
2. The plan's assets must be invested.

The written plan can be an IRS-approved master, an IRS-approved prototype plan offered by a sponsoring organization (bank, trade or professional organization, insurance company, or mutual fund), or an individually designed plan that has been approved by the IRS. The requirements and procedures for investing plan assets are defined within the written plan. (See IRS Publication 4222, *401(k) Plans for Small Business*, for additional investment guidance.)

Contributions

On an annual basis, employers must pay enough into the plan to satisfy the minimum funding standard under a money purchase pension plan or a defined benefit plan. As stated earlier, satisfying the minimum funding standard is complicated and may require professional guidance. (See IRC §412 and its regulations for further information.)

In general, a qualified plan is funded by employer contributions; however, some written plans may permit employees to make contributions. Deductible contributions may be made for a tax year up to the due date of the employer's return (plus extensions) for that year. (Employer's promissory notes made out to the plan are not deductible.)

Self-employed individuals cannot make contributions for themselves in tax years when they do not have net earnings from self-employment in the trade or business for which the plan was set up—even if they contribute for employees.

Contribution Limits —Defined Benefit Plans

For 2015, the annual benefit for a participant under a defined benefit plan cannot exceed the lesser of the following amounts:

> 100% of the participant's average compensation for his or her highest three consecutive calendar years; or
>
> $210,000 ($210,000 for 2016 as well).

Contribution Limits —Defined Contribution Plans

For 2015, a defined contribution plan's annual contributions and other additions (excluding earnings) to the account of a participant cannot exceed the lesser of the following amounts:

> 100% of the compensation actually paid to the participant; or
>
> $53,000

Employee Contributions

Participants may be permitted to make nondeductible contributions to a plan in addition to those made by the employer. Even though these employee contributions are not deductible, the earnings on them are tax-free until distributed. (See IRC §401(k) and §401(m) and IRS Notice 98-1 in *IRS Cumulative Bulletin 1998-1*.)

Deduction Limits

The deduction limits for a qualified plan depend on the type of plan and whether the individual is self-employed.

Profit-Sharing and Money Purchase Pension Plans

A business owner may deduct the amount contributed to a plan up to a limit of no more than 25% of the employee's compensation paid during the year.

Defined Benefit Plans

The deduction limits for defined benefit plans are based on actuarial assumptions and computations. Consequently, an actuary must figure the employer's deduction limit.

Multiple Plans

If a business owner contributes to more than one type of qualified plan and at least one employee is covered by both plans, the deduction for those contributions is limited to the greater of the following amounts:

- ☐ 25% of the compensation paid to the participating employees during the year;
- ☐ 100% of contributions to a defined benefit plan, provided that this amount is not more than the year's minimum funding standard for any of the qualified plans.

Self-Employed Individuals

See IRS Publication 560, *Retirement Plans for Small Business*, Chapter 5, *Rate Table for Self-Employed* or *Rate Worksheet for Self-Employed*, to calculate the maximum deduction that self-employed individuals can claim for qualified plan contributions made for themselves.

Nonqualified Plans

Qualified retirement plans can restrict the amount of benefits a higher-paid employee can receive; therefore, nonqualified plans are becoming extremely attractive. A nonqualified plan simply means that the retirement or deferred compensation plan does not comply with the Code's provisions that make employer's contributions deductible. Thus, the contributions that the company makes are not deductible until they are included in an employee's taxable income. This can be very useful, especially if the business is in a low tax bracket.

Because the plan is nonqualified, the discrimination rules governing qualified plans no longer apply. The plans can therefore favor key employees. Further, the compensation rules also do not apply, making nonqualified plans a must for high-income business owners.

Advantages of nonqualified plans include:

☐ Nonqualified plans do not have to cover every employee;

☐ No compensation, benefit, or contribution limits other than an overall reasonableness test;

☐ These plans require minimal bookkeeping and there are few reporting requirements.

However, nonqualified plans do have certain disadvantages:

☐ Benefits are unsecured promises to pay;

☐ Assets that may be intended for the payment of benefits must remain general assets of the company that are subject to the claims of creditors;

☐ Employer doesn't receive a tax deduction until the benefits are actually paid to the covered employees or are included in employees' income.

Business Structure Limitations

Table 16
Authorized Retirement Plans

Business Structure	SEP	SIMPLE IRA	SIMPLE 401(k)	KEOGH	401(K)
• Sole Proprietorship	YES	YES	NO	YES	NO
• Partnership	YES	YES	NO	YES	NO
• Limited Liability Company	YES	YES	NO	YES	NO
(any of the above with employees other than owner)	YES	YES	YES	YES	YES
• S corporation	YES	YES	NO	NO	NO
(with non-owner employees)	YES	YES	YES	YES	YES
• C corporation	YES	YES	YES	NO	YES

Individual Retirement Accounts

Traditional Individual Retirement Accounts (IRAs)

A traditional individual retirement account (IRA) is any IRA that is not a Roth IRA or a Simple IRA. Changes in the tax law concerning IRA contribution limits and eligibility requirements have made traditional IRAs an attractive option for retirement savings. (See IRS Publication 590, *Individual Retirement Arrangements (IRAs)*, Chapter 1, *Traditional IRAs*.)

Taxpayers can have a traditional IRA whether or not they are covered by any other retirement plan. However, deductions for IRA contributions may be limited if the taxpayer is covered by an employer retirement plan. (See *Phase Out Limits* in this section.)

Contributions to traditional IRAs are deductible and grow on a tax-deferred basis. Distributions are subject to tax. However, taxpayers can withdraw funds from their IRAs to pay college or post-graduate expenses and up to $10,000 to buy a first home without being subject to an early withdrawal penalty.

Contribution Limit

The most that an individual can contribute to his or her traditional IRA is the smaller of the compensation earned during the year or $5,500 in 2015. (Compensation includes wages, salaries, commissions, self-employment income, alimony, and separate maintenance.) There is also an annual catch-up contribution for taxpayers age 50 and older. In 2015 these taxpayers can contribute an additional $1,000, for a total contribution of $6,500.

Regardless of the number of IRAs set up by an individual, these limits apply to the total contributions made to all IRAs for the year (including Roth IRAs, but excluding employer contributions made under a SEP or SIMPLE IRA plan).

Spousal IRA Limit

Special IRA contribution limits apply to spouses who file joint returns. Within income limitations, a nonworking spouse can also make a deductible contribution to his or her own traditional IRA up to $5,500 in 2014, or $6,500 if the spouse is over the age of 50. (See IRS Publication 590, *Individual Retirement Arrangements (IRAs)*, Chapter 1, *Traditional IRAs*.)

Phase-Out Limit

Employees who actively participate in an employer-sponsored retirement plan may be entitled to only a partial (reduced) deduction for traditional IRA contributions, or no deduction at all. The deduction begins to decrease (phase out) when the taxpayer's modified adjusted gross income (AGI) rises above a certain amount.

In the year 2015 eligibility for IRA deductions is not completely phased out until AGI hit $71,000 for single filers or $118,000 for joint filers (same in 2016). However, a nonparticipant spouse may make a deductible IRA contribution, as long as the couple's AGI s less than $193,000 ($194,000 in 2016). (See IRS Publication 590, *Individual Retirement Arrangements (IRAs)*.)

 Although deductions may be reduced or eliminated, IRA contributions can still be made up to the general limit ($5,500 [or $6,500 if the taxpayer is over the age of 50] or 100% of compensation, whichever is less) or the spousal limit, if it applies.

Roth IRAs

A Roth IRA is an individual retirement plan that is generally subject to the same rules that apply to a traditional IRA, except in two key respects:

1. Contributions to a Roth IRA cannot be deducted.
2. Qualified distributions from a Roth IRA account are received tax-free.

Roth IRAs continue to gain in popularity because the financial advantages of receiving tax-free distributions are often perceived to be greater than those that are associated with deducting contributions.

To be a Roth IRA, the account or annuity must be designated as a Roth IRA when it is set up. Neither a SEP-IRA nor a SIMPLE IRA can be designated as a Roth IRA.

Contribution Limit

If contributions are made only to Roth IRAs, a taxpayer's contribution limit generally is the compensation earned during the year up to $5,500 in 2015 and 2016 (or $6,500 if the spouse is over the age of 50). However, more complex limitations are imposed if contributions are made to both Roth IRAs and traditional IRAs. In addition, the allowable contribution to a Roth IRA is subject to phase-out rules that are based on the AGI of the taxpayer. (See IRS Publication 590, *Individual Retirement Arrangements (IRAs)*, Chapter 2, *Roth IRAs*.)

☑ Regardless of the number of IRAs set up by an individual, the contribution limit applies to the total contributions made to all IRAs for the year (including Roth IRAs, but excluding employer contributions made under a SEP or SIMPLE IRA plan).

Conversion to a Roth IRA

Taxpayers may convert an existing IRA (traditional, SEP, or SIMPLE IRA) to a Roth IRA. The conversion is treated as a complete distribution for income tax purposes. In other words, the distribution will be taxed as income. However, the conversion will not be subject to an early withdrawal penalty. (See IRS Publication 590, *Individual Retirement Arrangements (IRAs)*.)

Health Savings Accounts (HSAs)

Health savings accounts (HSAs) are accounts that are set up with a qualified HSA trustee to enable taxpayers to pay certain medical expenses. These accounts must be used in conjunction with a high-deductible health plan (HDHP). In addition, the taxpayer must not have other health coverage (with certain exceptions), cannot be enrolled in Medicare, and cannot be claimed as a dependent by another taxpayer.

HDHP Deductible Limits

The law establishes the minimum annual deductible as well as the maximum out-of-pocket expenses for HDHPs.

Table 17
2015 High-Deductible Health Plan (HDHP) Limits

Contribution and Out-of-Pocket Limits for Health Savings Accounts and High-Deductible Health Plans			
	For 2016	For 2015	Change
HSA contribution limit (employer + employee)	Individual: $3,350 Family: $6,750	Individual: $3,350 Family: $6,650	Individual: no change Family: +$100
HSA catch-up contributions (age 55 or older)*	$1,000	$1,000	No change**
HDHP minimum deductibles	Individual: $1,300 Family: $2,600	Individual: $1,300 Family: $2,600	Individual: no change Family: no change
HDHP maximum out-of-pocket amounts (deductibles, co-payments and other amounts, but not premiums)	Individual: $6,550 Family: $13,100	Individual: $6,450 Family: $12,900	Individual: +$100 Family: +$200

* Catch-up contributions can be made any time during the year in which the HSA participant turns 55.

** Unlike other limits, the HSA catch-up contribution amount is not indexed; any increase would require statutory change.

Employer Contributions

Contributions made to a qualified individual's HSA are exempt from federal income tax withholding, social security tax, Medicare tax, and FUTA tax, up to annual dollar limits. The maximum limits that can be contributed to an HSA depend upon the type of HDHP coverage you have.

Note: A taxpayer does not have to put any money into his or her HSA. Employer contributions to an employee's HSA up to the maximum tax-exempt limit are 100% tax deductible by the employer. The employee does not have to pay income tax on the amount contributed, but the employee cannot claim the above-the-line deduction on contributions made by an employer. In addition, savings earned on all HSA contributions accumulate tax-exempt.

Distributions

In general, HDHPs require the insured to pay medical expenses during the year without being reimbursed until the annual deductible limit is reached. The HSA participant who has adequate deposits in his or her HSA can ask the trustee for distributions to cover these and other qualified medical expenses as defined in IRS Publication 502, *Medical and Dental Expenses.*

Distributions that are not used for qualified medical expenses are taxed as income when received and incur a 20% additional tax penalty. However, there is no additional tax if the participant is disabled, age 65 or older, or dies during the year.

Flexibility

Participant Options

Participants are not required to ask for HSA distributions to cover medical expenses. They can save what they do not spend on medical care by leaving the funds in their HSAs. In either case, HSA investment earnings accumulate tax-exempt.

Self-Employed Options

For the self-employed, HSAs are the most radical health-care reform since World War II. First of all, a self-employed individual generally finds that the premiums are significantly lower for a HDHP. This allows them to contribute the rest of their health premium budget into their own 100% tax-deductible HSA (up to the limits discussed in this section). The HDHP premiums are 100% deductible to self-employed individuals. Further, barring a major medical expense, the MSA can be used as a very effective way to reduce taxes and accumulate tax-exempt savings. (See IRS Publications 15-B, *Employer's Tax Guide to Fringe Benefits*, and 969, *Health Savings Accounts and Other Tax-Favored Health Plans*.)

Health Reimbursement Arrangements (HRAs)

A Health Reimbursement Arrangement (HRA) allows an employer to reimburse an employee's qualified medical expenses. Employees are not allowed to contribute to their own HRA. The employer makes contributions to the HRA, up to a maximum dollar amount, and the employee uses the funds to reimburse his qualified medical expenses. Reimbursements can be made for the medical expenses of the employee, the employee's spouse, and the employee's dependents. The balance in the HRA is allowed to accumulate and doesn't need to be withdrawn during the tax year.

For C corporations, the contributions are deductible by the employer, and they are not included in gross income by the employee.

Sole proprietors cannot participate in a Health Reimbursement Arrangement directly, but if the sole proprietor hires his or her spouse as a bona fide employee, the spouse can be covered by an HRA. The HRA can then be used to reimburse the medical expenses of the spouse, the sole proprietor, and their dependents. The sole proprietor can deduct the HRA contributions as a business expense, and the spouse does not have to include the contributions in gross income.

A 2% or more shareholder of an S corporation can participate in an HRA, but the shareholder's W-2 will include the value of the contributions in income subject to federal and state income tax. The contributions will not be subject to social security, Medicare, and FUTA taxes. The shareholder can deduct his health insurance premiums as an above-the-line deduction, and can deduct the qualified medical expenses as itemized deductions. The S corporation can deduct the HRA contributions as a business expense.

A partner in a partnership can also participate in an HRA. If the payments are for services rendered by the partner, the partnership will deduct the contributions as guaranteed payments. The partner will include the contributions in income subject to income tax and self-employment tax, and the partner can take an above-the-line deduction for the contributions. If the contributions are distributions (not payments for services), they are neither deductible by the partnership nor includible in the partner's gross income. The partner can take the above-the-line deduction to arrive at adjusted gross income on his individual income tax return.

(See IRS Publication 15-B, *Employer's Tax Guide to Fringe Benefits*, and IRS Notice 2008-1, *Special Rules for Health Insurance Costs of 2-Percent Shareholder-Employees*.)

The Affordable Care Act (ACA) also made changes to HRAs. Most notably, you cannot use an HRA to reimburse individual market coverable. The Department or Labor and the IRS have issued conflicting guidance for employers, so I will not address the specifics in this book; rather, make sure to contact a professional for advice on using an HRA.

APPENDIX

Useful Tax Information

Possible Business Deductions

It is unlikely that any one business would be eligible to claim all possible deductions. However, any business can deduct customary and reasonable expenses, which may include many of those listed here.

Accounting & bookkeeping	Advertising
Assistants	Airplanes, boats
Automobiles	Business seminars
Business licenses	Books
Bad debts (also consider debt to you)	Business consultants
Bonuses	Burglar alarm systems
Commission paid to salesmen	Convention & hotel expenses
Certified audits	Charitable contributions
Contract labor	Copyrights
Dividend exclusion	Directors fees
Depreciation	Disability plans

Depletion	Dues to professional organizations
Electricity	Entertainment (50% deductible)
Finder's fees	Filing expenses
Fire arms, ammunition (for business security)	Financial consultants
Fire/flood/hurricane losses	General business insurance
Internet	Interest
Invoicing	Insurance
Incorporating costs	Limited partnership costs
Life insurance	Local transportation
Losses in business	Logos
Legal fees	Maintenance
Medical reimbursement plan	State industrial insurance
Newspapers, magazines	Office equipment
Pension plans	Public relations
Professional literature	Printing
Postage	Patents
Repairs	Records
Travel	Tips, gratuities
Theft losses	Training programs, courses
Trademarks	University, further education

Partnerships

☐ A partnership has no separate income tax rate. Profits and losses are passed through to the partners on Schedule K-1 and are taxed on the individual partner's tax return.

☐ Every partnership must file Form 1065, an informational return, regardless of the amount of income or loss. If the partnership does not receive income and does not incur any expenses, the partnership is not required to file a return.

- ☐ Filing deadline: April 15th.
- ☐ Schedule K-1: A partnership is required to furnish Schedule K-1 to each partner by the due date of the partnership tax return.

C Corporations

- ☐ C corporations must file a Form 1120 regardless of the amount of income or loss. It must file even if it stops conducting business.
- ☐ Estimated tax: A corporation must make estimated tax payments.
- ☐ Filing deadlines following the close of the C corporation's tax year:

Fiscal Year End Filings
1st Payment — 15th day of the 4th month
2nd Payment — 15th day of the 6th month
3rd Payment — 15th day of the 9th month
4th Payment — 15th day of the 12th month

Calendar Year End Filings
1st Payment — April 15th
2nd Payment — June 15th
3rd Payment — September 15th
4th Payment — December 15th

C Corporation Tax Rates
Form 1120

Taxable Income		Tax	
Over	Not Exceeding	$s + % of amount over:	
$0	$50,000	$0 + 15%	$0
$50,000	$75,000	$7,500 + 25%	$50,000
$75,000	$100,000	$13,750 + 34%	$75,000
$100,000	$335,000	$22,250 + 39%	$100,000
$335,000	$10,000,000	$113,900 + 34%	$335,000
$10,000,000	$15,000,000	$3,400,000 + 35%	$10,000,000
$15,000,000	$18,333,333	$5,150,000 + 38%	$15,000,000
$18,333,334 and above		35% flat tax rate	

Personal service corporations — 35% flat tax rate

S Corporations

- ☐ An S corporation must file a Form 1120S regardless of the amount of income or loss. It must file even if it stops conducting business. An S corporation's profit or loss is passed through to shareholders and reported on the shareholders' Schedule K-1.
- ☐ Filing deadline: March 15th.
- ☐ Estimated tax: Shareholders are responsible for payment of estimated tax on their tax returns.

Estates, Trusts, and Gifts

If you give money or property to someone during your life, you may be subject to federal gift tax. When you die, the money and property that you own (your estate) may be subject to federal estate tax.

Most gifts are not subject to the gift tax and most estates are not subject to the estate tax. For example, there is usually no tax if you make a gift to your spouse or if your estate goes to your spouse at your death. If you make a gift to someone else, the gift tax does not apply until the value of the gifts you give that person is more than the annual exclusion for the year. Even if tax applies to your gifts or your estate, it may be eliminated by the "unified credit."

Generally, you do not need to file a gift tax return unless you give someone, other than your spouse, money or property worth more than the annual exclusion for that year. An estate tax return generally will not be needed unless the estate is worth more than the applicable exclusion amount for the year of death. This amount is shown in the table titled *Unified Credit for Estate and Gift Taxes*.

The recipient of your gift or your estate will not have to pay any gift tax or estate tax. Also, that person will not have to pay income tax on the value of the gift or inheritance received.

Making a gift or leaving your estate to your heirs does not ordinarily affect your federal income tax. You cannot deduct the value of gifts you make (other than gifts that are deductible charitable contributions).

Unified Credit

A credit is an amount that eliminates or reduces tax. A unified credit applies to both the gift tax and the estate tax. You must subtract the unified credit from any gift tax that you owe.

> Any unified credit you use against your gift tax in one year reduces the amount of credit that you can use against your gift tax in a later year.
>
> The total amount used against your gift tax reduces the credit available to use against your estate tax.

In 2015, the unified credit eliminated taxes on a total of $5,430,000 (applicable exclusion amount) of taxable gifts and taxable estate ($5,450,000 for 2016).

Gift Tax

The gift tax applies to the transfer by gift of any property. You make a gift if you give property (including money), or the use of or income from property, without expecting to receive something of at least equal value in return. If you sell something at less than its full value or if you make an interest-free or reduced interest loan, you may be making a gift.

The general rule is that any gift is a taxable gift. However, there are many exceptions to this rule. Generally, the following gifts are ***not taxable*** gifts:

- ☐ Gifts that are not more than the annual exclusion for the calendar year
- ☐ Tuition or medical expenses you pay for someone (the educational and medical exclusions)

- ☐ Gifts to your spouse
- ☐ Gifts to a political organization for its use
- ☐ Gifts to charities

Annual Exclusion

A separate annual exclusion applies to each person to whom you make a gift. For 2014-2016, the annual exclusion is $14,000. Therefore, you generally can give up to $14,000 each to any number of people and none of the gifts will be taxable.

If you are married, both you and your spouse can separately give up to $14,000 to the same person in 2015 without making a taxable gift. After 2016, the $14,000 annual exclusion may be increased due to a cost-of-living adjustment. See the instructions for Form 709 for the amount of the annual exclusion for the year you make the gift.

Filing a Gift Tax Return

Generally, you must file a gift tax return on Form 709 if any of the following apply:

- ☐ You gave gifts that are more than the annual exclusion for the year to someone (other than your spouse).
- ☐ You and your spouse are splitting a gift.
- ☐ You gave someone (other than your spouse) a gift that he or she cannot actually possess, enjoy, or receive income from until sometime in the future.
- ☐ You gave your spouse an interest in property that will be ended by some future event.

Estate Tax

Estate tax may apply to your taxable estate at your death. Your taxable estate is your gross estate less allowable deductions.

Gross Estate

Your gross estate includes the value of all property in which you had an interest at the time of death. Your gross estate also will include the following:

- ☐ Life insurance proceeds payable to your estate or, if you owned the policy, to your heirs;
- ☐ The value of certain annuities payable to your estate or your heirs;
- ☐ The value of certain property you transferred within three years before your death.

Taxable Estate

The allowable deductions used in determining your taxable estate include:

- ☐ Funeral expenses paid out of your estate
- ☐ Debts you owed at the time of death
- ☐ The marital deduction (generally, the value of the property that passes from your estate to your surviving spouse)

See Form 706 and its instructions for more information on what is included in your gross estate.

Applying the Unified Credit to Estate Tax

Basically, any unified credit not used to eliminate gift tax can be used to eliminate or reduce estate tax.

Filing an Estate Tax Return

An estate tax return, Form 706, must be filed if the gross estate, plus any adjusted taxable gifts and specific gift tax exemption, is more than the filing requirement for the year of death.

> *Note*: An adjusted taxable gift is the total of the taxable gifts you made after 1976 that are not included in your gross estate. The specific gift tax exemption applies only to gifts made after September 8, 1976, and before 1977.

Filing deadline: Within 9 months of death.

Filing requirement: In 2015, the filing requirement is for estates with gross values of $5,430,000.

Estate & Gift Tax Rates

 Here is the top marginal estate and gift tax rate schedule:

Year	Exclusion Amount
2006–08	$2,000,000
2009	$3,500,000
2010–11	$5,000,000
2012	$5,120,000
2013	$5,250,000
2014	$5,340,000
2015	$5,430,000
2016	$5,450,000

Personal Income Tax Rates

Tax brackets for individuals in 2014 are as follows:

Married Individuals Filing Joint Returns and Surviving Spouses

If Taxable Income Is:	The Tax Is:
Not over $18,150	10% of the taxable income
Over $18,150 but not over $73,800	$1,815 plus 15% of the excess over $18,150
Over $73,800 but not over $148,850	$10,162.50 plus 25% of the excess over $73,800
Over $148,850 but not over $226,850	$28,925 plus 28% of the excess over $148,850
Over $226,850 but not over $405,100	$50,765 plus 33% of the excess over $226,850
Over $405,100 but not over $457,600	$109,587.50 plus 35% of the excess over $405,100
Over $457,600	$127,962.50 plus 39.6% of the excess over $457,600

Unmarried Individuals
(other than Surviving Spouses and Heads of Households)

If Taxable Income Is:	The Tax Is:
Not over $9,075	10% of the taxable income
Over $9,075 but not over $36,900	$907.50 plus 15% of the excess over $9,075
Over $36,900 but not over $89,350	$5,081.25 plus 25% of the excess over $36,900
Over $89,350 but not over $186,350	$18,193.75 plus 28% of the excess over $89,350
Over $186,350 but not over $405,100	$45,353.75 plus 33% of the excess over $186,350
Over $405,100 but not over $406,750	$117,541.25 plus 35% of the excess over $405,100
Over $406,750	$118,118.75 plus 39.6% of the excess over $406,750

APPENDIX

Business Tax Strategies

Business Structure

Consider whether your current form of business is still best for you.

Income and Expenses

- ☐ To the extent possible, shift income into next year and accelerate deductions.
- ☐ Buy business supplies at the end of a profitable year and accelerate other expenditures like repairs and maintenance.
- ☐ Buy equipment before the end of the year to take advantage of Section 179 expense deductions.
- ☐ Review entertainment, club dues, and meal expense accounts.

- ☐ Switch to an "accountable" plan if you are currently reimbursing employee business expenses under a "nonaccountable" plan.

- ☐ Donate excess inventory to qualified charities to receive larger deductions.

- ☐ Conduct a cost segregation study to identify and price real property (i.e., buildings) separately from nonstructural items and land improvements in order to accelerate depreciation.

Compensation

- ☐ Consider a compensation and fringe benefit study to see what makes sense tax-wise. For example, "split the difference" on compensation increases by providing benefits that are deductible by the company, but tax-free to the employee.

- ☐ Avoid payroll taxes by shifting a portion of compensation from salary to fringe benefits. (Unreimbursed medical expenses and payroll-deducted group insurance are ideal benefits to include in a fringe benefit cafeteria plan.)

- ☐ Set up a cafeteria plan to allow employees to pay for their dependent care expenses. This will likely save them more than they would receive from the childcare tax credit.

- ☐ Review the status of workers as employees or independent contractors to make sure they are correctly classified.

Tax Deferral

- ☐ Establish a 401(k) or SIMPLE program to help attract and retain quality employees.
- ☐ Set up a nonqualified retirement plan for your highest paid key employees.

Family Employees

- ☐ Deduct 100% of the health insurance premiums for your spouse and dependents if you are self-employed and employ your spouse in your business.
- ☐ Employ your children if you own your own business to take advantage of several tax benefits.

Notes

1. The most recent statistics are available on-line at *www.irs.gov*. The annual Data Book (usually Publication 55B) contains statistics ranging from tax revenues collected to tax revenues collected per return audited.
2. The audit data used for the book was via the IRS yearly report was for 2014.
3. See endnote #1.
4. Audit rate for "C" corporations with total assets less than $250,000—0.4%; for "S" corporations—0.40%; for partnerships—0.4%; and for individuals (non-schedule C filers) earning $50,000 to $100,000—0.4%.
5. Under the example illustrated on the previous page, the "No Change Rate" for the individual scrutinized by a revenue agent would have been 5%, while the "C" corporation, "S" corporation and partnership's would have been 35%, 36%, and 44% respectively.
6. IRS Collections, "Table 6—Internal Revenue Gross Collections, by Type of Tax, Fiscal Years 1960-2014."
7. *U.S. Master Tax Guide*, CCH, Inc., 1992: 184.
8. IRC, §469(e)(1).
9. IRC, §469(c)(1).
10. Remember- "deductible" means that the expense is subtracted from your total, or gross, income. What is left is referred to as your "net profit" or "earnings."
11. Based on the IRS Data books, the audit rates for schedule C filers earning $100,000 is typically four times greater than those of other business entities.
12. This is an allowable deduction for self-employed individuals. (See Schedule SE, Line 6.)
13. There are constant proposals in Congress to eliminate estate taxes (a.k.a. death taxes). I have included the estate tax schedule in the appendix of this book for easy reference.

14. The fiscal year (tax year) of most partnerships is December 31; therefore, the return would be due by midnight on March 15. See IRS Publication 541 for more details.
15. 1986 Tax Reform Act
16. Interstate means activities that cross state lines versus intrastate where activities occur primarily within one jurisdiction. For example, an Internet company whose customers are all over the US would be interstate in nature, while Mom and Pop's Grocery down the street would be intrastate.
17. 1986 Tax Reform Act.
18. IRC §448.
19. Ibid.
20. Doctors and other professionals' corporations fall within the category of a personal service corporation (PSC) and profits are taxed at a flat 35%.